Titles by *Langaa* RPCIG

Francis B. Nyamnjoh
Stories from Abakwa
Mind Searching
The Disillusioned African
The Convert
Souls Forgotten
Married But Available
Intimate Strangers

Dibussi Tande
No Turning Back. Poems of Freedom 1990-1993
Scribbles from the Den: Essays on Politics and Collective Memory in Cameroon

Kangsen Feka Wakai
Fragmented Melodies

Ntemfac Ofege
Namondo. Child of the Water Spirits
Hot Water for the Famous Seven

Emmanuel Fru Doh
Not Yet Damascus
The Fire Within
Africa's Political Wastelands: The Bastardization of Cameroon
Oriki'badan
Wading the Tide
Stereotyping Africa: Surprising Answers to Surprising Questions

Thomas Jing
Tale of an African Woman

Peter Wuteh Vakunta
Grassfields Stories from Cameroon
Green Rape: Poetry for the Environment
Majunga Tok: Poems in Pidgin English
Cry, My Beloved Africa
No Love Lost
Straddling The Mungo: A Book of Poems in English & French

Ba'bila Mutia
Coils of Mortal Flesh

Kehbuma Langmia
Titabet and the Takumbeng
An Evil Meal of Evil

Victor Elame Musinga
The Barn
The Tragedy of Mr. No Balance

Ngessimo Mathe Mutaka
Building Capacity: Using TEFL and African Languages as Development-oriented Literacy Tools

Milton Krieger
Cameroon's Social Democratic Front: Its History and Prospects as an Opposition Political Party, 1990-2011

Sammy Oke Akombi
The Raped Amulet
The Woman Who Ate Python
Beware the Drives: Book of Verse
The Wages of Corruption

Susan Nkwentie Nde
Precipice
Second Engagement

Francis B. Nyamnjoh & Richard Fonteh Akum
The Cameroon GCE Crisis: A Test of Anglophone Solidarity

Joyce Ashuntantang & Dibussi Tande
Their Champagne Party Will End! Poems in Honor of Bate Besong

Emmanuel Achu
Disturbing the Peace

Rosemary Ekosso
The House of Falling Women

Peterkins Manyong
God the Politician

George Ngwane
The Power in the Writer: Collected Essays on Culture, Democracy & Development in Africa

John Percival
The 1961 Cameroon Plebiscite: Choice or Betrayal

Albert Azeyeh
Réussite scolaire, faillite sociale : généalogie mentale de la crise de l'Afrique noire francophone

Aloysius Ajab Amin & Jean-Luc Dubois
Croissance et développement au Cameroun :
d'une croissance équilibrée à un développement équitable

Carlson Anyangwe
Imperialistic Politics in Cameroon:
Resistance & the Inception of the Restoration of the Statehood of Southern Cameroons
Betrayal of Too Trusting a People: The UN, the UK and the Trust Territory of the Southen Cameroons

Bill F. Ndi
K'Cracy, Trees in the Storm and Other Poems
Map: Musings On Ars Poetica
Thomas Lurting: The Fighting Sailor Turn'd Peaceable / Le marin combattant devenu paisible
Soleil et ombre

Kathryn Toure, Therese Mungah Shalo Tchombe & Thierry Karsenti
ICT and Changing Mindsets in Education

Charles Alobwed'Epie
The Day God Blinked
The Bad Samaritan
The Lady with the Sting

G. D. Nyamndi
Babi Yar Symphony
Whether losing, Whether winning
Tussles: Collected Plays
Dogs in the Sun

Samuel Ebelle Kingue
Si Dieu était tout un chacun de nous ?

Ignasio Malizani Jimu
Urban Appropriation and Transformation: bicycle, taxi and handcart operators in Mzuzu, Malawi

Justice Nya' Wakai
Under the Broken Scale of Justice: The Law and My Times

John Eyong Mengot
A Pact of Ages

Ignasio Malizani Jimu
Urban Appropriation and Transformation: Bicycle Taxi and Handcart Operators

Joyce B. Ashuntantang
Landscaping and Coloniality: The Dissemination of Cameroon Anglophone Literature

Jude Fokwang
Mediating Legitimacy: Chieftaincy and Democratisation in Two African Chiefdoms

Michael A. Yanou
Dispossession and Access to Land in South Africa:
an African Perspevctive

Tikum Mbah Azonga
Cup Man and Other Stories
The Wooden Bicycle and Other Stories

John Nkemngong Nkengasong
Letters to Marions (And the Coming Generations)
The Call of Blood

Amady Aly Dieng
Les étudiants africains et la littérature négro-africaine
d'expression française

Tah Asongwed
Born to Rule: Autobiography of a life President
Child of Earth

Frida Menkan Mbunda
Shadows From The Abyss

Bongasu Tanla Kishani
A Basket of Kola Nuts
Konglanjo (Spears of Love without Ill-fortune) and
Letters to Ethiopia with some Random Poems

Fo Angwafo III S.A.N of Mankon
Royalty and Politics: The Story of My Life

Basil Diki
The Lord of Anomy
Shrouded Blessings

Churchill Ewumbue-Monono
Youth and Nation-Building in Cameroon: A Study of
National Youth Day Messages and Leadership Discourse
(1949-2009)

Emmanuel N. Chia, Joseph C. Suh & Alexandre Ndeffo Tene
Perspectives on Translation and Interpretation in
Cameroon

Linus T. Asong
The Crown of Thorns
No Way to Die
A Legend of the Dead: Sequel of *The Crown of Thorns*
The Akroma File
Salvation Colony: Sequel to *No Way to Die*
Chopchair
Doctor Frederick Ngenito

Vivian Sihsbu Yenika
Imitation Whiteman
Press Lake Varsity Girls: The Freshman Year

Beatrice Fri Bime
Someplace, Somewhere
Mystique: A Collection of Lake Myths

Shadrach A. Ambanasom
Son of the Native Soil
The Cameroonian Novel of English Expression:
An Introduction

Tangie Nsoh Fonchingong and Gemandze John Bobuin
Cameroon: The Stakes and Challenges of Governance and
Development

Tatah Mentan
Democratizing or Reconfiguring Predatory Autocracy?
Myths and Realities in Africa Today

Roselyne M. Jua & Bate Besong
To the Budding Creative Writer: A Handbook

Albert Mukong
Prisonner without a Crime: Disciplining Dissent in
Ahidjo's Cameroon

Mbuh Tennu Mbuh
In the Shadow of my Country

Bernard Nsokika Fonlon
Genuine Intellectuals: Academic and Social
Responsibilities of Universities in Africa

Lilian Lem Atanga
Gender, Discourse and Power in the Cameroonian
Parliament

Cornelius Mbifung Lambi & Emmanuel Neba Ndenecho
Ecology and Natural Resource Development
in the Western Highlands of Cameroon: Issues in Natural
Resource Managment

Gideon F. For-mukwai
Facing Adversity with Audacity

Peter W. Vakunta & Bill F. Ndi
Nul n'a le monopole du français : deux poètes du
Cameroon anglophone

Emmanuel Matateyou
Les murmures de l'harmattan

Ekpe Inyang
The Hill Barbers

JK Bannavti
Rock of God *(Kilàn ke Nyùy)*

Godfrey B. Tangwa (Rotcod Gobata)
I Spit on their Graves: Testimony Relevant to the
Democratization Struggle in Cameroon

Henrietta Mambo Nyamnjoh
"We Get Nothing from Fishishing", Fishing for Boat
Opportuies amongst Senegalese Fisher Migrants

Bill F. Ndi, Dieurat Clervoyant & Peter W. Vakunta
Les douleurs de la plume noire : du Cameroun
anglophone à Haïti

Laurence Juma
Kileleshwa: A Tale of Love, Betrayal and Corruption in
Kenya

Nol Alembong
Forest Echoes (Poems)

Marie-Hélène Mottin-Sylla & Joëlle Palmieri
Excision : les jeunes changent l'Afriaque par le TIC

Walter Gam Nkwi
Voicing the Voiceless: Contributions to Closing Gaps in
Cameroon History, 1958-2009

John Koyela Fokwang
A Dictionary of Popular Bali Names

A Dictionary of Popular Bali Names

John Koyela Fokwang

Langaa Research & Publishing CIG
Mankon, Bamenda

Publisher:
Langaa RPCIG
Langaa Research & Publishing Common Initiative Group
P.O. Box 902 Mankon
Bamenda
North West Region
Cameroon
Langaagrp@gmail.com
www.langaa-rpcig.net

Distributed outside N. America by African Books Collective
orders@africanbookscollective.com
www.africanbookscollective.com

Distributed in N. America by Michigan State University Press
msupress@msu.edu
www.msupress.msu.edu

ISBN: 9956-616-47-8

© John Koyela Fokwang 2010
First Published 1986
Second edition published in 1992

DISCLAIMER

All views expressed in this publication are those of the author and do not necessarily reflect the views of Langaa RPCIG.

Contents

Dedication .... *vii*
Acknowledgment .... *ix*
Foreword .... *xi*
Preface to Third Edition .... *xiii*

Introducing the Dictionary 1

A	25
B	28
C	36
D	37
F	40
G	42
I	46
J	47
K	49
L	54
M	57
N	60
O	71
P	72
S	75
T	78

V	80
W	82
Y	84
Z	86

Wedding Names 87
Equivalents of Chamba and English Names 88
Common Names 92
    Common Insects 92
    Common Reptiles 97
    Common Animals 99
    Common Birds 105
    Common Plants and Fruits 110

Dedication

To my late parents

Na Esther Killa Fokwang
Ba Francis Kambem Fokwang

Acknowledgment

It is my sincere hope that this dictionary of Bali names will serve the purpose for which I have taken the pains to write. The names have been arranged alphabetically and their meanings provided. It is hoped that users will easily find the meanings of their favourite names from the alphabetical order. For the first time, an index of themes has been provided which could also assist users in their search for names relevant to their specific contexts. The background information provided in the introduction provides very important context to the origin and derivation of names. As will be detailed shortly, the names owe their origin in Mubako, the original language of the Chamba people and Mungaka, the current language of Bali Nyonga.

My deep gratitude for encouragement goes to Na Juliana Kaboh Langsi, and Ba Tita Gwandiku C F of Jamjam Quarter in Bali; Mr and Mrs John Fombutu of Playfair Bookshop, Bamenda; Messrs Peter Gana, Peter Sama Salle, Sama Nyonga Peter and all members of Nda Ngwe Wum for the great part they played towards the realisation of the first edition of this work.

I acknowledge with gratitude the part played by my wife, Mrs Emerentia Andin Fokwang in taking good care of me and our children during the time I spent in researching and producing this dictionary. I am equally thankful to Dr Elias M Nwana who laboriously read through the manuscripts, corrected and gave suggestions which greatly improved the quality of this work and above all, accepted to write a foreword.

Many thanks go to all those who have given me feedback from the first edition and thus enabled this second edition to be what it is. I wish to extend special thanks to Mr Kohla Nyongbega Daniel of PDA, Statistics, Bamenda and the

Bali Kumbad elements who knit and sell traditional gowns by the Cultural Centre Bamenda. I still ask for corrections and suggestions for improvement and additional names with their meanings for future editions of this book.

**Fokwang John Koyela
Bamenda, 1992**

Foreword

The Nature, Design and Purpose of this Book

I am highly honoured to be asked to write a foreword to Mr Fokwang John Koyela's book entitled ***The Dictionary of Bali Popular Names***. This is not the first time a work in Bali popular names is appearing in public. It first appeared in December, 1981 with the title ***The Living Culture of Bali Nyonga***, a collection of some popular names together with a pictorial presentation of some aspects of the Bali Culture edited by Mr Augustine F Ndangam and myself. As was acknowledged in that edition, the collection of popular names was largely the work of Mr Fokwang John Koyela.

The dictionary of Bali popular names is an enlarged and improved edition of Mr Fokwang's first work. In this edition, hundreds of other new popular names given to children in Bali with their meanings have been added, to enrich the book.

The names in this book have been arranged alphabetically together with their language of origin, sex and meanings. The two main origins of Bali popular names are Mubako the original language spoken by all the Bali Chamba people of the North West Province of Cameroon. A second source of these names is the "Mungaka language", now spoken by the Bali Nyonga people of the North West Regons, Cameroon.

This book begins with an introduction describing the Southward movement of the Bali Chamba people from their original home in the River Benue to their present sites. This is immediately followed by the rituals of naming a child in Bali Nyonga, with an explanation of how some of the names have been derived.

Mr Fokwang has to be praised for putting into the hands of many Bali people such a working document as a dictionary of Bali popular names. Bali people the world over can now find the meanings of their own names with ease from this dictionary or can select suitable names for their new born children from the book. The names of Bali Nyonga week days as well as the names of the lunar months in Bali have been spelt out here. Priests and Pastors who formerly refused to baptise people bearing Bali traditional names for lack of the meanings of these names may now do so. Researchers in Bali culture may find in this book some similarities in popular names between the Balis of the Northwest Province of Cameroon and those of their kith and kin in Northern Cameroon and Northern Nigeria.

There is no better way of serving a people than committing into print those aspects of their culture that have survived the ages for the next generation. By writing the dictionary of Bali popular names, Mr. Fokwang is preserving for the coming generation some aspects of the living cultures of the Bali people. It is hoped that other researchers in Bali culture will follow suit.

Dr Elias M. Nwana
Bamenda, 1992

Preface to Third Edition

What is really in a name? Names are markers of one's identity in society. Naming is a cultural universal, meaning that all human societies name their members. In some societies, elaborate rituals tend to accompany the naming of new members – often at birth. But names are not only acquired at birth. In many African societies and elsewhere, people continue to acquire names throughout their lives, sometimes marking the different transitions they undergo in life. These important events are sometimes known as "life crisis" moments and tend to be accompanied with "rites of passage". The attainment of full personhood in many societies is often characterised by changes in one's appellation. A common example is the acquisition of a regal name at the coronation of a new king. In many societies of the Cameroon grasslands, adult members of society acquire new names when they are chosen to "succeed" departed members of their families. This is a potent illustration of the claim that ancestors are not completely dead and forgotten but are indeed the living-dead; they live or re-live in the persons that bear their names. They also live on in the names of remembrance that are transmitted from generation to generation exemplified by names such as Babila which translates into "father has returned".

This preface has been written many months after the death of Mr John Koyela Fokwang, the author and pioneer researcher on names and naming rituals among the Chamba of the Northwest region of Cameroon. A passionate researcher and teacher throughout his life, Mr Fokwang began researching Chamba names in the early 1980s, all at his personal expense. His research took him to Bali Kumbad where Mubako, the original language of the Chamba is still spoken. He was intrigued to learn that despite the fact that

Bali Nyonga had embraced a new language during their migration in the mid 19th century, they had nevertheless retained Chamba names, while of course adopting new ones from neighbours and faraway lands thanks to their entrepreneurial disposition.

Following his retirement from the Cameroon civil service, John Fokwang turned his focus back to his initial academic passion – researching Chamba names. His intension was to publish a third edition of his now famous dictionary but his dreams were compromised by the cold hands of death on April 19 2009. Diagnosed with cancer in early 2008, he hastened to revise the dictionary including other academic projects he had embraced during his teaching and administrative career. During the revision, he sought to include the following additions in the third edition; first, a section detailing common names of birds and animals in Mungaka which he reckoned would be of tremendous benefit to both adults and younger generations. Secondly, he sought to investigate a dozen or so names whose meanings had eluded him during previous research sessions. Then, finally he also intended to provide clarification for a series of names with ambiguous or contentious meanings, particularly those with supposedly negative connotations.

On account of his failing health he achieved only the first of the above three objectives. Hence, this edition contains a list of common animals and plants. This list is far from exhaustive and we have included only those whose meanings he was able to establish in the course of his research. We have ensured that where possible, photos of these items are available to match. This will ensure that learning is made easier for users of any level. We will continue to update the list as data become available and see to it that future editions of this dictionary contain a much longer list of common animals and birds. This edition is therefore a tribute to his legacy. It is also published at this time to coincide with the first anniversary of his transition.

It also needs to be highlighted that some of the names whose meanings we have been unable to establish have been removed in this edition. Research will continue to be carried out and it is our intention to provide their full meanings in a future edition. However, we have substantially revised the grammar of the meanings of most names in this volume while remaining faithful to the spirit of the original meanings. Most names are provided literal meanings but sometimes literal interpretations can be misleading. Names tend to stand for something; in other words they are also metaphors that describe or represent a range of possibilities or circumstances. We have endeavoured to conceptualise what these possibilities are and stretched their meanings to include modern/contemporary dispositions. Let us illustrate this point with an example; **Fongwen** is a popular name given to a male child born on Ntungwen (a week day in the local calendar) or at the farm. A century ago, the farm represented an area of primary economic activity. Today, many people of Bali descent are involved in other economic activities besides farming so a child born in the «farm» or at one's job site can be metaphorically named Fongwen. This point is buttressed by the fact that many Mungaka speakers in the diaspora (domestic and transnational) tend to refer to their jobs (nursing, administrative, teaching, etc) as farm work. In this context, the «farm» becomes a key symbol from which a range of activities are associated and names derived.

Let us end this preface by addressing an issue of debate that remains contentious to this day. It is the question regarding whether names shape or determine in some way one's personality or destiny. Clearly, there are belief systems that uphold the view that names carry more than just their ordinary meanings; that they are closely tied to their bearers' personality and for these individuals any attempt to challenge this belief would be sacrilegious. Our position is that names should not be perceived as imbued with some kind of spell over their bearers. Although certain individuals may feel their names have influenced their bearing and social standing in life, it is our understanding that this contradicts the principle of free will and an affront to individual and collective agency. Parents and other name givers may choose specific names on the conviction or belief that such names would bring good luck to their bearers. As stated earlier and as will become obvious in successive sections of this volume, individuals choose certain names for a variety of reasons. Names may mark the new social status of the giver (he or she may have enjoyed a rich harvest for example) rather than the bearer while in certain contexts chosen names may speak to the parents' aspirations (or anxieties) for their child.

We are critically aware of the challenge in putting together a dictionary of this sort for a modern readership. Improvements have been made and will continue to be modified as new data are gathered. For instance, we have changed the layout in this edition compared to previous ones and for the first time, an index has been created which allows users to search for specific names based on themes. We wish to encourage users to spice up their naming ceremonies by drawing on customary practices recounted in this dictionary. Individuals are also encouraged to invent their own rituals insofar as these activities are imbued with profound meaning for everyone involved. Husbands may wish to add a touch of romance to their matrimonial life by choosing wedding names for their wives that appeal to their particular contexts. This suggestion stands irrespective of how long a couple has been married. It is in this light that a new section devoted to wedding names has been added. For those who still prefer Christian names, it is important to keep in mind that equivalents of these names are available in Chamba languages and that many Christian denominations now accept members to be baptised with

African or indigenous names insofar as these names do not contradict the Christians principles they profess. It is our hope that this dictionary goes a long way in preserving and promoting our collective heritage. We reckon that you will find this edition much easier to use.

Jude Fokwang, PhD
Lilian Ndangam Fokwang, PhD
Toronto, Canada
January 2010

Introducing the Dictionary

The quest for education, employment and the intermingling of cultures have led Bali people to different parts of Cameroon and abroad. Today, we have huge settlements of Bali subjects in the North America, Europe, Asia and other parts of the world. Many of them have married and celebrated the birth of their children in these lands. Many have also opted to name their children with African names, sometimes alongside Christian or European names. The challenge for these immigrants is what the precise meanings of these names are – conscious of the symbolic significance these names hold for both their bearers and givers. In fact some even hold the view that certain names are associated with good fortune.

Unlike in pre-colonial times when only authorised elderly persons in one's family could name a child, Bali subjects, like everyone else living in the modern world are expected to name their child upon his/her birth in order to meet the official requirements of birth registration. This means that the rituals often associated with naming as it were have not only been eroded by modern exigencies, but also forgotten by many people of Bali descent. But what is yet to become a key asset is a dictionary of Bali names – a classified pool of knowledge and names from which people of Bali descent or friends of Bali can readily draw from in the service of family duties and for general knowledge.

This dictionary seeks to fill this huge gap. I have undertaken this arduous task, at tremendous personal expense to collect Bali names, arrange them alphabetically and provided their meanings based on extensive field research in Bali Nyonga and Bali Kumbad. The dictionary also provides a guide to users that directs them to the socio-cultural contexts under which particular names may be chosen for a child.

It is also my intention that this volume will help whoever is charged with the responsibility of naming children in his/her family to do it properly so that the riches of our names and culture can be preserved for posterity. I should emphasise that in the past, several factors were often taken into account when naming a child. It wasn't only the beauty of the name as it were, or its meanings but more precisely, the specific circumstances, events and challenges faced by the expecting parents/family before the birth of the child. As it will become obvious to the user, the names have both literal and proverbial meanings. Tremendous caution should be observed that names, particularly those that apparently have "negative" meanings are not misunderstood for "doom" or Bali people's predilection for things negative. Some of these meanings speak to the circumstances surrounding the birth of an individual which in consequence serves as a historical reminder of the challenges a given family has faced over the ages.

This third edition incorporates a number of changes from the previous ones. First, more names have been added and the meanings of certain names which were left out have been provided. In general, the meanings of all names have been revised, updated and articulated in simple plain English. An appendix from the second edition has been retained which contains English names, their meanings as well as their equivalents in Mungaka or Mubako. It is intended that this list of English names and their equivalents will assist Christian parents in choosing names for their children for the purposes of baptism. This edition also has a new layout format; as it is the first time it has been edited on a computer. The table format of the previous editions has been replaced with a conventional dictionary layout. Another addition is an index which will help expedite the process of a name search thematically or by specific words. Lastly, a new section provides the names of common birds, animals and plants/fruits in Mungaka. Where possible, illustrations of these items are also provided which will serve as a tremendous educational tool for children and adults.

A Short History of the Chamba

The exact origin of the Chamba is not clear but oral traditions maintain that they migrated from East Africa via Sudan and settled in the North between what is presently known as Nigeria and Cameroon. At their settlement near the River Benue they founded the Dindi Kingdom and mingled with the Puli Mbatsu' (Red lip Fulani), and taught them how to use bows and arrows. In the eighteenth century famine and occasional Fulani raids led by Adama forced the Chamba to leave their settlement in the Adamawa region towards the south (see Nkwi & Warnier 1982). During their migration southwards they incorporated the Buti-Kontcha, Nabuli, Balede and the Buti Suga groups into their Kingdom.

On reaching Adamawa, they settled east of Ngaoundere where some Tikar groups joined them to form a Chamba raiding group of mounted-bow men to which the name "Ba'ni" was given. They camped in Wiya Clan and carried raids in the area, among which included Bui's old capital of Kovifem. They continued their movement eastwards and incorporated the Kufads and ended up in Banyo where more Tikali and Buti people joined them.

Due to unknown reasons, the Chamba broke into two groups. One led by Gyanda moved north westwards towards Takum while the other led by Gawolbe, son of Ga Gangsin moved to the Bamenda area. The Chamba continued to raid the areas they travelled through and upon arrival in Ngie, Gawolbe's contingent set up a war camp. Here, some of the raiding parties enjoyed momentary success, while their counterparts who ventured into Mundani and southern Moghamo met with a stiff counter attack. A joint group mounted a massive raid at Bakem-Bafu Fundong near present-day Dschang where they lost more horses and their leader Gawolbe. The death of Gawolbe caused a split of the Chambas into several contingents. Ganyama led the Mudi contingent northwards through Bamenda to form the Benue Chamba. Part of Ganyama's followers settled in a village now in the Furu Awa District in Menchum Division. Galanga led his group and founded Bali Gham[1], now in the Santa municipality. Galabe founded Bali Kumbad, Gavabi founded Bali Gangsin and Gayam founded Bali Gashu – all in Ndop region. Nyongpasi son of Princess Nyonga founded Bali Nyonga. Bali Kohntan whose leader is not known settled at the present site occupied by Bali Nyonga but was incorporated into the latter group on account of their numerical and military strength.

Nyongpasi led his contingent to Bamum where he launched an abortive invasion of the kingdom. He and his followers were expelled but took along with them, the Batis, Wons, Kundems, Fulengs, Munyams, Ngiams, Sangams, Sets, Ngods, Laps and the Ndiangs and crossed the River Nun to acquire their present site. The Bakohs (Bawocks) and the Kumjas migrated later and settled with the Bali Nyonga people. Today all the incorporated people form the major population of Bali Nyonga and are referred to as *Banten* or *Lo'Lo* people.

Naming among the Bali

Bali Nyonga currently has a population of about 80.000, occupying an area of 192 sq km. It is probable that Bali is the most heterogeneous kingdom in the Cameroon grassfields on account of the diverse clans and ethnic groups that constituted the area at the time it was founded in the nineteenth century. Many of these sub-groups have retained their names and some of their leaders occupy sub-chieftaincies in the kingdom. In some parts of Bali, elderly

---

1. This area is also known in certain texts as Bali Bagam.

members still express themselves in their respective languages besides Mungaka which serves as the unifying language.

Naming in Bali Kumbad, Bali Gham, Bali Gangsin, and in Bali Gashu is done in Mubako, the original language of the Chamba but in Bali Nyonga, Mubako and Mungaka names as well as those with Metta, Set, Mughamo, Tikali, Buti, Kundem, Ngod, Won, etc, derivations are found. This qualifies the claim made above that Bali Nyonga remains a deeply heterogeneous kingdom.

A general survey of the names reveals that among the Bali, children are named depending on the social circumstances, events and challenges faced by the expecting parents. Most names speak to the existing conditions and future aspirations of the family. Sometimes, names are derived from current events such as ritual holidays, days of the week, some months of the year, or popular Chamba symbols such as the spear and fig tree. Other key symbols from which names are fashioned include but are not limited to love, God, fire, cutlass (machete), leopard, death, the earth or soil, evil, enmity, mat, medicine and above all, family or one's homeland.

Symbols in Chamba Names

What are symbols? The American anthropologist, Sherry Ortner distinguishes between two kinds of symbols, summarising and elaborating symbols. The former is relevant to our work and will therefore be employed as a working definition. For her, "Summarizing symbols, first, are those symbols which are seen as summing up, expressing, representing for the participants in an emotionally powerful and relatively undifferentiated way, what the system means to them. This category is essentially the category of sacred symbols in the broadest sense, and includes all those items which are objects of reverence and/ or catalysts of emotion – the flag, the cross, the churinga, the forked stick, the motorcycle, etc" (Ortner 1973: 1339-

40). Based on this understanding of symbols, I therefore proceed to identify some of the key symbols among the Chamba upon which many names are derived.

(a) Spear
The spear is central to the production and articulation of manhood and masculinity among the Chamba. Prior to the adoption of guns, hunting and warfare were conducted with spears. Armed with a spear, a man was perceived as providing protection to his wards. Without a spear, a man cannot stand his enemy but armed, he is said to be ready for any challenge. A common name derived from «spear» is Dinga which literally means a spear. Hence in summary, the spear symbolises protection, strength and manhood.

(b) Fig Tree
Another key symbol among the Chamba is the fig tree. By virtue of the fact that the fig tree hardly withers even during the long dry season, it represents for the Chamba, the sign of continuity or a line of succession. The fig tree is planted when a son establishes a new compound. The presence of a fig tree therein signifies the continuity of the lineage and the collective aspiration for growth from generation to generation. A common name derived from this is Gima, which literally means fig tree.

(c) Death
Death remains the ultimate mystery faced by human beings. It is a mystery yet to be fully understood or resolved. Intrigued by its inevitability, some families name their children after recent deaths or events surrounding the death of a member of the lineage. Clearly, names that relate to death are most controversial and need to be treated with caution. The rationale of choosing names informed by the theme of death should be understood in symbolic terms; they represent specific kinds of idioms through which people

try to make sense of bereavement. Sometimes, the names are intended to mock at or ridicule death (man's eternal enemy). Names derived from the theme of death include, Bohbad and Valla.

(d) Mouth
The mouth is the principal organ through which speech is articulated. It is central to human communication. Among the Chamba, the mouth is perceived as an organ that has the potential to unite or divide people. It could make or mar and as such should be used with care. A name derived from this is Guka'a.

(e) Earth
The earth is the ultimate provider of all the resources we need to survive. The Chamba believe that human beings are made of "the earth" or dust and shall eventually return to it. The earth is sacred in Chamba cosmology and generally enjoys a positive meaning. Names derived from the earth tend to be given to children on account of events that relate to the soil or land. Examples of such names include Yebba, Kehyeba.

(f) Mats
In pre-colonial times – and probably during the long migratory journeys of the Chamba people, mats were valued only for sleeping on. Upon settling at the present site, mats became valued as objects for decorating the gates of titled persons. Today they are used for drying food items, interior decorations, and other uses suitable to their owners. Names from this group include; Kidla, Vakidla.

(g) Leopard [Tiger]
Tigers aren't indigenous to Africa but the Chamba tend to refer to the leopard as tiger (probably due to a translation error dating from colonial times). However, both animals belong to the cat family and are highly valued for their skin.

Among the Chamba, the leopard's skin signifies elegance and royalty. Ownership and disposal of these skins have been monopolised by the powerful kings of the region. Parents tend to name their children after the leopard in the hope that the child will bring a good name to the family. Names derived from this symbol include Gua and Bidgua.

(h) Family
Human beings are by their very essence social beings. The family is central to their social organisation and constitutes the basis for society. The Chamba believe that family support is critical to anyone's success in life. In their worldview, there is no place for anyone without a family – or put differently, no one can exist without a family. Hence, the family serves as a powerful source of names, e.g. Bisangha, Bidbilla.

(i) Problems
There is no family, or people without challenges. Challenges include family disputes, ill-luck, gossip, natural disasters etc. Sometimes, the Chamba name their children after events or issues that are informed by the challenges they face. It needs to be emphasised that names that bear the traces of "problems" are not in themselves bearers of problems but rather constitute the memories of these events. Alternatively, some of the names are intended to serve as potent forces acting against the challenges faced by parents or members of the family at a given point in time. Some of the names derived from this include; Nyonga and Nunyonga.

Days of the Week
Like in most kingdoms of the Cameroon grassfields, the Bali Chamba groups have an eight-day week cycle. This contrasts quite distinctly with the Judeo-Christian week cycle of seven days or other African regions (e.g. the Igbos) that have a four-day week cycle. In essence, the diversity inherent in regional calendars and week cycles reveals that time is a product of

culture not an act of nature or rather that time tends to be constructed independent of natural patterns. This point is echoed by the French sociologist, Emile Durkheim who maintains that "The division into days, weeks, months, years, etc., corresponds to the recurrence of rites, festivals, and public ceremonies at regular intervals. A calendar expresses the rhythm of collective activity while ensuring that regularity." The eight days of the Bali weekly cycle include:

Ngo
The day *ngo* (termites) are hunted or the day Ngu dancers hold their weekly meetings. Names derived from this include; Fongo, Ndango, Fongu.

Ndansi
This is the day the *Nsi* society holds its meeting. Male children born on this day may be named Ndansi.

Nkohntan
The eve of the Bali customary market day when neighbouring villages especially those from the southern forest zone trekked to Bali town in order to conduct business the following day. It is the day reserved on the customary calendar when a bride is escorted to her bridegroom's compound. An example of a name derived from this is Nkohntan.

Ntanbani
This is the name for the Bali market day. Names that originate from this include; Ninantan and Mantan.

Foncham
This is the customary day of obligation or rest, known popularly in the Cameroon grassfields as Kontri Sunday. Farming, the principal economic activity in this region is taboo on such a day. A common name derived from this is Foncham.

Ntungwen
The day people are permitted by custom to resume regular economic activity e.g. farming. Names derived from this include Ntungwen and Fongwen.

Ntanbutu
This is the customary market day of the Mbutu people often massively attended by people from Bali town. An example of a name derived from this day is Fombutu.

Dzimbufung
This is the customary day of obligation or rest of the Mbufung people, a subgroup in Bali Nyonga. Mbufung is a small village where most Bali residents own large tracts of farmland. Whereas the people of Mbufung observe this day as a day of rest, it is for residents of Bali Nyonga a market day. A common name derived from this is Fofung.

Week Days in Bali Chamba Chiefdoms

Bali Nyonga	Bali Gham	Bali Kumbad	Bali Gangsin	Bali Gashu
Ngo	**Nyamginma**	Mallisella	Gashu Sella	**Gashu Sella**
Ndansi	Tankah	Kwangamba	**Mukongsella**	Mbolibang
Nkohtan	Munjensella	**Ngotia**	Ngotia	Ngotia
Ntanbani	Ngumbaa	Balangsella	Nyamloba	Nyam-nieba
Foncham[2]	Selgwah	Bapiyid	Nyamgingwa	Nyamsella
Ntungwen	Yenteh	Nyamginna	Fanjisella	Fanjisella
Ntanbutu	Yencap	Baforkyidlo	Messingsella	Nyamgingwa
Dzimbufung	Seljemaa	Selpna	Selpna	Gahforkyidlo

---

2. This is the traditional day of obligation - known popularly as kontri Sunday. Expressed in Judeo-Christian terms, it is a day of rest.

NB: Those in bold denote the market days of the respective villages. Except for Bali Nyonga, the days have not been arranged on the basis of the regular week day sequence.

Months

Unlike the Julian or Gregorian calendars that have cycles of 12 months each, the Bali Chamba calendar has thirteen months, calculated according to local cosmology through the observation of the moon's movements. The first phase of a moon is always watched with great anticipation. Certain months have specific customary activities or festivals attached to them from which certain names are derived;

1. Sodza – Sodza
2. Sonia – Nahsua
3. Sodzela
4. Soduna
5. Sogamba
6. Buluwa
7. Sagwaa
8. Gwansoa – Nahsona
9. Sosakea
10. Vomsoa – Nahvoma, Voma, Nwana etc.
11. Sogebba
12. Lehsoa – Nahlela
13. Sosasia

Besides the above categories, naming among the Chamba can be summarised as follows:

Names of Deceased parents

It is customary among the Chamba to name children after parents who have died. This practice is rooted in elementary beliefs about reincarnation and accords with African ancestor worship which elevates the ancestors to the realm of the living-dead. In this sense, the ancestors are believed to be present among the living. For the Chamba, it is crucial to remember them through new generations by naming new members with the names of deceased lineage members. For instance, Babila or Billa is a typical name given to a male child born after the death of his grandfather. On the other hand, Nahbila is given to a female child born after the death of her grandmother. Modified versions of this practice consist in naming children after the specific «names» borne by deceased grandparents.

Compound Names

There are several compound names formed either by combining two separate names or using prefixes. While some of the compound names have figurative meanings, others retain their literal meanings. An example of a compound name is the combination of Dinga and Bobga which gives Dingbobga or Bobdinga.

Teknonyms

Sometimes, names are fashioned out of the combination of a regular name and a title of respect. On becoming parents, some adults and grandparents are addressed by teknonyms – that is, names that refer indirectly to their (grand)children (see below). Among the Chamba, it is an honour to be addressed by teknonyms and such names are sometimes given to newborns upon the passing of their original bearers.

Ma: Dinga's mother becomes Madinga.
Ka: Doh's grandmother becomes Kadoh.
Doh: Feh's grandfather becomes Dohfeh.
Ta: Fongo's father becomes Tafongo.

Honorific Names

Like in most chiefdoms of the grassfields, age is an important marker of social organisation. Individuals also attain social distinction upon becoming parents or when they are conferred titles of honour on account of their unique contribution to the welfare of the chiefdom. The Balis are widely known to uphold the custom of respect for one's elders or seniors through the use of certain titles such as Ni or Ma that have gained wide currency beyond the grassfields. The following titles are noteworthy;

General

- ***Ni:*** This tends to be used in isolation or as a prefix to a person's names when addressing a male person identified as one's senior. It is not customary for children to address their parents with this title or the female equivalent, ma. Ni is also employed by one's peers to denote mutual respect.

- ***Ma:*** This title is used for females in similar manner as Ni described above.

Familial

- ***Ba:*** This refers to father. It is employed when addressing one's father or male persons in one's father's age group. The title of Ba is also employed in reference to one who succeeds his father or inhertis the position of lineage head.

- ***Na:*** This refers to mother. It is employed when addressing one's mother or female persons in one's mother's age.

- ***Kah:*** Means grandmother. It is used as a sign of respect to one's paternal or maternal grandmother.

- ***Nimbang:*** This title means uncle. Precisely, it is employed when addressing one's mother's brother although it is often used in a generic sense to mean uncle.

Bambot: Paternal uncle. Father's junior brother
Nambot: Maternal aunt. Mother's junior sister
Bannguket: paternal uncle. Father's older brother.
Nanguket: Maternal aunt. Specifically the elder sister of one's mother
Tangwi: This means aunt. Its precise use is with reference to one's father's sister – that is, a paternal aunt.
Doh: This means grandfather. It is used as a sign of respect to one's grandfather.

Royalty and other Notables

Mooh: This title is used when responding to a male person who has assumed the title of Tita, Sama or has been elevated to the rank of a sub-chief.
Ndeh: This title is used when addressing a Nkom or any fully recognised member of the Ngumba cult.
Mbeh/Chabafon: This title is used solely when addressing the king or responding to the king's call.
Tita: This is a title of respect reserved for a prince.
Mboe: This is a title of respect reserved for a princess.

Titled Names

These are names that identify specific families or lineages. Such names are generally considered as family or surnames in a Western sense and are borne by one's offspring and successive generations. Non-family members are not permitted by custom to give such names to their children. For instance a class of names that are borne by members of specific families include some of the titled names of the Komnfon. Komnfon are the king's councillors. In Bali, there are seven titled names that serve as markers of specific families or lineages. These titles cannot be withdrawn or reclaimed by the king. These include;

Tita Kuna, Tita Gwandiku, Gwancheleng, Gwaabe, Gwananji, Gwanyebit and Gwandi.

These councillors are headed by Tita Kuna, assisted by Tita Gwandiku. The titles of Komnfon are normally prefixed by Gwan. The following were the Nkoms in Bali Nyonga at the time of the book's second edition in 1986[3];

Gabana, Gwananji, Gwanbidnyonga, Gwanbobga, Gwanbobmuga, Gwanbulla, Gwanbumla, Gwancheleng, Gwandi, Gwandiku, Gwandima, Gwandingbe, Gwanfogbe, Gwangaduna, Gwangwaa Gwanjegana, Gwankobe, Gwankudvalla, Gwangkwangbe, Gwanlegbe, Gwanlima, Gwanmesia, Gwanmusia, Gwannua, Gwannulla, Gwannoghubea, Gwanpadinga, Gwanpua, Gwansadla, Gwansadnyonga, Gwansoduna, Gwanvalla, Gwanwua, Gwanyalla, Gwanyama, Gwanyella, Gwanyetulla and Gwankudla.

NB: It is generally ill-advised for the children of the above titled names to bear them as "surnames" even though a growing number of these titled men have fallen into the trap of turning these into surnames. This is ill-advised because such titles can be reclaimed by the king if a title-holder's successor is not deemed worthy of the title's honour.

Tita

This means prince. However, anyone who has risen within the ranks of local society or who leads a group may be awarded the title of Tita. For instance, Tita Kuna and Tita Gwandiku bear the title of Tita on account of their leadership positions among the Komnfon. Tita Gwenjeng and Tita Kung also bear the title of Tita as leaders of the Gwe cult.

Other bearers of the Tita title include the following;

---

3. A comprehensive list of all notables is currently being compiled and would be published in the next edition.

Tita Sama - leader of the princes.
Tita Sikod - the prince enthroned simultaneously with the king.
Tita Nyangang - leader of the Lela flag bearers.
Tita Gwanvoma - leader of the Voma Society.

Sama

This is the name generally given to a male twin. However, a male subject who has undertaken a cleansing ritual and attained a state of "purity" may be awarded the title of Sama.[4] Someone honoured with the title of Sama is also allowed by custom to initiate Lela.[5]

Nwana

This means rain, peace maker or a special, consecrated person. As an ordinary name, it is given to male children delivered in the month of Vomsoa or during the Voma festival. As a title, it is conferred as a mark of distinction for public service. Seven Nwanas make up the Voma cult.

Gwe

This is the name of the trickster scouts who guard the Lela flags during the Lela festival. They are also charged with the maintenance of public order during this festival. Other activities of the Gwe consist in entertaining the crowds. Gwe is also a prefix to their titles, e.g. Gwejeng, Gwepamuga, Gweningum, Gwelalab, etc.

Tutuwan

This is the title given to the standard bearers who carry the Lela flag and other insignia during the Lela festival.

---

4. Needs some elaboration.
5. Pob lela.

Nji
This title is derived from the Bamum kingdom. It is borne by some subchiefs, (Mfontes) and reputable palace retainers (Nchinteds).

Succession
Succession to hereditary titles in Bali especially 'ghangtshubu' (compound heads) is patrilineal and differs remarkably between the Banten and the Yani groups. However, the mfontes and others share common features. The latter are installed with some or all of the following:

i. **Nkoeti**- a fraternal deputy.
ii. **Tamfon** - his elder.
iii. **Mulla(h)** - his appointed retainer (in charge of pages) who is his nephew (mundzad).
iv. **Fomungwi** - she is the queen sister or princess. The Fomungwi is provided with a compound with an open gate near the palace.
v. **Mamfon** (Ka-nina) – she is the king's natural mother who is also provided with a compound and is allocated a female councillor (nkom Ka).
vi. **Suufon** - is a representative wife.

Foreign Names
It is clear from the short history of the Bali Chamba that they incorporated many groups during their long migration from what is present-day northern Cameroon to their present locations in the grassfields. They also welcomed other groups who sought their protection and were ready to live amicably with them (e.g. the Bawock in Bali Nyonga). Some of these sub-groups still retain their names although it is difficult to establish the extent to which they transmit these names to their children. A few cases have been recorded of parents who name their children with ancestral names but which are not recorded in birth certificates.

In pre-colonial times and during the colonial period, many Bali men were known in the region as renowned traders who travelled long distances to buy and sell local or foreign products. Such trips took many days to accomplish. Thus it was common practice for the traders to lodge in villages along their trade routes. Some of these men married wives from these villages and some even took up names after these areas or named their children after these villages. In fact, it became a popular trend for some of the traders to be named after the towns they had visited during their trading trips. Some of the names include; Mayuka for Muyuka, Victoa for Victoria, Makumba for Kumba, Nguti for Nguti, Akwa, Malende, Mamfe, Bassa and Ntali, Mbanga. Other names from such trade routes include: Ajong, Nobagen and Musi. Those who worked with or served the colonial officials bore names like Fineboy, Goodboy, Scott, Cleanboy etc.

Besides the importation of the names listed above, , Bali men also introduced foreign musical genres such as the Nchibi and Ngwe from the Keyaka people of Manyu Division, Kihdeng from the Moghamo and Lung or Kongi from the Metta.

Birth Rituals

Among the Bali Chamba, the home is considered central in the organisation of social life. It is in essence, the heart of the family and the primary locus of ritual action. For instance, a newborn's placenta (*lengmon*) and the remains from his/her navel (*ntongmon*) must be ritually buried at his/her father's family compound. Although this custom is not fully enforced in the contemporary era, it could be the subject of deep tensions in the past. A mother who gave birth outside the chiefdom and failed to repatriate the *ntongmon* to her husband's compound could be accused of infidelity. It was suspected that her failure to repatriate the *ntongmon* was a clear indication that the child did not belong to her husband's lineage. Clearly, the consequences for such a woman or her marriage were grave. People of Bali descent are encouraged to carry on with this custom but sanctions such as the above suspicions no longer hold.

In line with the belief system of the Bali, failure to repatriate a child's navel to his/her father's family compound has certain negative implications. First, this means the child has been denied his/her natural right to be "planted" (or installed) in his/her ancestral compound. Such a belief made sense in a region where belonging is directly connected to the land. A child, symbolically planted in the soil of his/her ancestors receives the blessings of the family which in the strictest sense includes the living-dead (ancestors). On the contrary, popular belief holds that a child who traces descent to Bali but whose navel wasn't "implanted" in his/her family compound will grow up to be a vagabond, wondering about the world without any clear sense of direction. He/she upon reaching maturity will hardly think of home or care for his/her family. On account of this belief, one sometimes overhear parents admonishing an unsteady child as follows; "why do you behave as if a dog ate your navel?"

Having discussed the importance of planting the remains of a child's navel among the Bali, it is worth devoting a few lines to describing how this ritual implantation is carried out. It should be emphasised that this custom is popular with contemporary residents of Bali although a few expatriates, out of love for the customs of their ancestors insist on carrying this out when they return home. After child birth, the child's placenta is taken to his/her father's compound and wrapped in leaves of piper umbellatum known locally as *fu mumbod* and buried outside at the corner of the living room or near the kitchen door. A flat stone is then placed over it to prevent its removal by domestic animals such as dogs. The manner of disposal of the remains from the navel differs among the sub groups in Bali Nyonga.

However, what is common among all these groups is that the placenta and the remains of the navel of newborns are ritually buried in their father's compounds. In most families, the remains of the navel are placed on *fu mumbod* along with camwood and red palm oil poured over it. The contents are then wrapped and buried at the same site as the placenta. The family member charged with the performance of this ritual is the child's paternal aunt (tangwi) or a designated female relative who acts on behalf of the aunt. Sometimes this ritual is carried on the day the child is first taken out for presentation to the public.

The day a baby is first taken out of the house is a remarkable day in the life of the Bali child because he/she is given a special name (luK nkang) on this day. In Bali Nyonga, each family names a baby at his/her birth and a second name is given on the day he/she is first taken out and presented to the public. This event normally takes place at the convenience of the family, subject to the availability of *nkang* (corn beer). These names – the one given at birth and the second when he/she is ritually presented to the public plus the family or father's name enables each child to have three names. Usually, the *luK nkang* has a Mubako derivation and meaning while the first name, often of Mungaka origin is either situational or is based on the day or month in which he/she was born. The advent of Christian names has eclipsed the significance of the *luK nkang*. Clearly, this dictionary of Bali names is intended to contribute to the revival of some these rich cultural practices, particularly in the light of Christian trends to accommodate African names in baptismal rites.

The Ritual Disclosure of a new born
The ritual disclosure or presentation of a child is often a day of tremendous significance to the child and his/her extended family. The following account is a standard

description of how this ceremony was carried out in the past. It is obvious that no two rituals were carried out in the same manner, so readers should bear in mind that the actual practice of this ritual may have slight variations from this account.

Often invited to this event are the paternal and maternal kinspeople as well as the parents' friends. Once everyone is assembled in the family courtyard, the nursing mother comes out of the house carrying the baby. She is seated on a low stool beside a log of wood and a bottle of red palm oil – items that will be used for the ritual. A *tangwi* or her representative brings out a piece of wood glowing with fire. She then gets out a razor blade and cuts off some hair from the child's head. She places the hair on a couple of piper umbellatum leaves together with remnants of the navel. She then adds camwood and red palm oil and stirs the mixture. Next, she cuts several shoots of the *behnyamga* plant and warms them over the glowing fire after which she dips the leaves into the mixture and waves them in front of each attendee who in response turns his/her head anti-clockwise. Each attendee then cuts a bit of the leaves and drops it in the mixture. Then she rubs the back of each attendee's hand (left for females and right for male) with the mixture.

Once the above has been concluded, the mother then hands over the new born to the person appointed to name the child. He/she then dips two fig tree leaves in the bowl of *nkang* three times and sprinkles some of it on the earth as a libation to the gods. Once again, he/she dips the leaves three times and puts in the child's mouth while calling out the chosen name. This part of the naming ritual is concluded when the *mumbod* leaves are folded and buried beside the door post where the child's placenta had been buried. In some families it is hidden between the palm fronds of a palm tree or in the crevice of a wall or sometimes, near a plantain stalk.

The second part of the ritual outing is then continued. Carrying the baby once again, the nursing mother prepares to follow the procession led by the *tangwi* who presided over the naming ceremony. Armed with a cutlass representing a masculine tool or a hoe symbolic of a female tool the *tangwi* leads the way in a mimetic performance of how the various tools are used. The nursing mother follows closely behind carrying the baby. If the child is a male, he and his mother are followed by an archer who shoots her back with harmless arrows while they walk round the house three times. The archer is closely followed by male attendees carrying spears and possibly, guns (when available) symbolising the things a man will need in life to prove his manliness. In the case of a female child, the *tangwi* leads the way with a hoe while her female counterparts walk behind the nursing mother carrying *kedjas*, baskets and other farm tools used by women.

On completing the third round, the nursing mother enters the house and leaves the door ajar. The *tangwi* follows but stops at the threshold with a bowl of water facing the mother and her child. She then calls out the nursing mother's name (preferably her wedding name) thrice who remains mute. At the third call she throws the water at them. This act is believed to imbue the child with courage, that is, to face the rain fearlessly once his/her mother resumes her daily chores which may sometimes entail the child's exposure to the rain.

The rest of the ceremony is characterised by eating and drinking spiced by songs led by females and dance that invoke tunes pertaining to birth celebrations. On this day, the nursing mother is tabooed from eating meat because according to local beliefs, this would be a symbolic eating of the child's navel. At the close of the day's celebration, the tangwi or chief celebrant departs with the items used for the ritual - namely the log of wood and the remainder of the palm oil. If the mixture in the *mumbod* leaves was buried by a plantain stalk, she also has rights over the first plantain to ripen from this tree.

Clearly, this naming ritual is rich in symbolism, much of which has lost its significance or relevance to Bali people. At this event, the principles of masculinity and femininity are played out through the tools employed by men and women in their daily lives. These objects only represent the subsistence activities of most Bali people – at a time when farming was central to their economic life. Today, many Bali people are involved in a wide variety of jobs or economic activities – law enforcement, education, medicine, business, media, administration etc. Perhaps, this ritual could be revived with a tinge of creativity whereby participants employ items/tools that signify the diversity of professions available locally and beyond the borders of the chiefdom. This ritual also demonstrates the importance of certain members of the Bali family, such as the position of "father's sister" or *tangwi* who is expected to play a central role in the naming ritual – even though she may not be the namer. In Bali society, both men and women may be appointed to name a new born and the ritual deployment of this honorific role is most cherished by the Bali people. For the new born, this may be his/her first rite of passage, the acquisition of a social identity based on his/her disclosure to society. For the parents and their extended families, this event is not just a celebration of new life but also, particularly for first-time parents, a marker of their transition to full social adulthood. It is therefore befitting that such an event should end in merriment.

References

Ortner, Sherry B. 1973. On Key Symbols. *American Anthropologist* 75 (5):1338-1346.

Nkwi, Paul Nchoji, and Jean-Pierre Warnier 1982. Elements for a History of the Western Grassfields. Yaounde: Department of Sociology, University of Yaounde.

Alphabetical Order of Popular Bali Names

Abbreviations
Mub - Mubako
Mug - Mungaka
m - Male
f - Female

NB:

- Some names that end with **O** tend to be pronounced as in the schwa-sounded words in English; *urge*: /ɜːdʒ/ or *verge*: /vɜːdʒ/. In this dictionary, these endings are represented by the letter ō. An example of such a name is **Akambōwō**.

- Some names in Mubako tend to be shortened e.g. Langmi for Langmia, Nahva for Nahvalla; Yiva for Yivalla.

Abong, m, Mug
It is good or pleasant. Goodness, beauty, pleasing to behold.

Abongwō, m Mug
Who is better? Who is without blemish? The name is an acknowledgement of the claim that to err is human or simply put, no one is perfect.

Achaa-Achaa, m, Mug
It is simply above me. The challenge is beyond my competence. This is a challenge that has tested my ability.

Achowufawō, m, Mug
If you are deeply involved or implicated in a matter, to whom can you delegate or transfer your concern? Put alternatively, to whom can one delegate one's role in a given matter or situation?

Afanyikob, m/f, Mug
Literally, it means God has given. This is a gift from God. It is symbolic of a special or salutary gift filled with the promise of a prosperous and happy future.

Ajimbom, f, Mug
Who knows its maker? The name is also suitable for a wedding name in which context it means my wife who knows my wants. The name is also appropriate for a child whose mother has taken rather long before giving birth.

Ajinyikob, m/f, Mug
God knows. God is omniscient.

Ajiwō, m/f, Mug
Who knows? No one knows everything.

Akakō, m, Mug
What is it that we have not seen?

Akambu, m, Mug
It is not yet fruitful. It will ripen in due course. This name evokes a sense of profound anticipation.

Akambōwō, m, Mug
There is no person without challenges. Literally, who is without problems?

Akamdawō, m/f, Mug
There is no house without challenges. Every household or family has its own issues.

Akamduwō, m/f, Mug
No one is faultless. Imperfection is human or to err is human.

Akamya, m/f, Mug
Is there a place without challenges? Insofar as there is life, challenges will always present themselves.

Alahbi, m/f, Mug
Literally, it will eventually be fruitful. This refers to an issue of great promise.

Alanikō, m, Mug
How has this come about? This issue needs to be unravelled. This refers to an issue whose origin is yet to be ascertained.

Alobbub, m, Mug
Idiom; let it be so; may it enjoy stability. This seems to be an expression or desire for stability.

Alohmbōwō, m/f, Mug
What is its origin? Who is the author of this matter? This name tends to be given to a child whose father is unknown.

Alohmbōwu, m/f, Mug
Idiom; were you the one faced with this situation, what would you do?

Alohya, m/f, Mug
Where is it from? This name is synonymous to Alohmbowo. It expresses ambiguity, uncertainty and possibly, dismay. The context in which such a name is used remains ambiguous.

Anah, f, Mub
A thing, matter, issue, item.

Anbeh, f, Mub
This is a fresh gift, one without conditions. This is a generous gift without strings attached.

Andin(wō), f, Mug
Who would have predicted such an occurrence? The shorter version of the name, Andin is more popular although some prefer the full name Andinwô.

Anseh, m/f, Mub
He/she has or owes nothing.

Antebba, f, Mub
This refers to a cool thing or item. It is suitable as a wedding name in which case it means a calm and beautiful bride.

Atedmboyi, f, Mug
The matter is left in her hands. She is expected to assume full control of the issues facing her.

B

Babila, m, Mub
Father has come back. A male child is named Babila if he is born after the death of his grandfather. The feminine of this name is Nahbila. The name is often interpreted from the perspective of the new born's father who sees the symbolic "return" of his father in the new child.

Babongha, m/f, Mug
Be optimistic in life. Always find room for optimism in life.

Badjangman, f, Mug
A war fought to demonstrate superiority. This name is often given to a woman by a husband who eloped with her.

Badmia, m, Mub
He has amazed me. He has taken me by surprise.

Bafon, m, Mug
This name is derived from the root, fon which means king. The first male child born into a sub-chief's family upon his death is suitably named Bafon.

Banguket (Bauket), m, Mug,
Literally, this means a senior paternal uncle; (also see Bambod). This name is appropriate for a male child born after the death of his paternal uncle, particularly if his father is a junior to the deceased uncle.

Banwana, m, Mub
It is the plural of Nwana, which means peacemakers.

Baiina, m, Mub
This matter is above me.

Bakanu, m, Mug
Literally, it means a second encounter is not worthwhile. This name carries a deeper meaning which can be translated as once bitten twice shy.

Balahmbim, m, Mug
We shall agree. No matter how long it takes, we shall eventually come into accord.

Balahkan, m, Mug
We shall eventually be exhausted. Parents overwhelmed by challenges may name a child as such.

Bamua, m, Mub
Father is tired.

Bambod, m, Mug
Literally, this refers to a junior paternal uncle. Also see Banguket.

Bambubo, m, Mug
There is no caretaker.

Bangmia, m, Mub
This name has three distinct meanings; first, it means the matter is above me. Second, we have called you to explain an issue and lastly, we are thinking about the matter.

Banijeye, m/f, Mug
We are watching to see what will happen. Put differently, it means we are on the watch out for any eventuality.

Banikō, f, Mug
What do I owe you? In what way am I indebted to you?

Banla, m, Mub
It is above fire. This could also mean a non-flammable item that nevertheless may engender fire.

Banni/Banyina, m/f, Mub
This means an excess of something; Superabundance; excess.

Banyugga, m, Mub
I won't be annoyed even if you abuse me. I will maintain my calm even when confronted with insult; a cool-spirited person; one not easily driven to anger.

Banu, m, Mug
This means father of difficulties or problems. It could also mean trouble-shooter or someone equipped to deal with challenges.

Basung, m, Mug
Let us express our thoughts and minds to the fullest. This also means rumour-mongers are aplenty.

Baya, m, Mug
Where is father?

Behgha, m, Mub
I have seen it. This conveys a sense of inner consciousness on account of a physical or spiritual revelation.

Behnyonga, f, Mub
I have seen the wonders of life. It also means I have faced challenges in life.

Behseh, m/f, Mub
This name has two meanings; first, the voice of the people and second, he/she hasn't seen it.

Be, m/f Mub,
I have seen a stranger. See.

Bengyella, m, Mub
I have fastened my machete and can now declare myself a mature man. (NB: Machetes are associated with manliness in many chiefdoms of the grassfields).

Bidbila, m, Mub
The home has returned to normalcy. A family beset by challenges has once again found calm.

Bidbungha, m, Mub
Crystal. This refers to a matter that has crystallized, been clarified or fixed.

Bidgangha, m, Mub
This name has two meanings. First, it means you cannot penetrate the palace fence. Second, the village is determined to stand its ground.

Bidgoga, m, Mub
I won't metamorphose into an animal in order to avoid society's resentment. I would rather conform to society's expectations of me than turn myself into an outcast.

Bidgua, m, Mub
The village leopard. A person that commands respect and admiration.

Bidjenmia, m/f, Mub
People envy me.

Bidkunga, f, Mub
A relative can't be changed. Alternatively, it means one doesn't choose one's relative.

Bidlaa, m, Mub
The village fire. This symbolises warmth and comfort.

Bidlangmia, m, Mub
The village opposes me. I stand in opposition to the people. It also means I am surrounded or ambushed by the community.

Bidlola, f, Mub
It has become a matter of amusement and laughter. The child has forced a dispute between her parents to be settled. A child that enables the resolution of a crisis between her parents. A child's intervention that brings forth mirth and merriment.

Bidmia, f, Mub
An issue that has changed me.

Bidpenna, f, Mub
The village has improved. People have changed for the better.

Bidsona (Bisona), f. Mub
My home, family, or village is in a satisfactory state. All is well and good with my people.

Bidtola, m. Mub
The village has become bigger.

Bidyeba, f, Mub
An issue that has changed the order of things. Something that has brought about the transformation of the world. A major source of change.

Bidyebga, f. Mub
You can't change the earth. It also possibly means you can't change the world.

Bidyogha, f, Mub
It is a village issue. This also means an issue of public interest or concern.

Bikayi, m, Mub
It has been earmarked. Someone set apart for a particular purpose. A chosen one.

Billa, m, Mub
Father has been reborn. A symbolic reincarnation of one's father.

Bimmua, m, Mub
He is tired or bored.

Binnah, m/f, Mub
Loosened, unfastened or released. Symbolises an open-minded person.

Binseh, m, Mub
A thing that remains fastened; yet to be released. Possibly, it means someone whose potential is yet to be appreciated. See Binnah for an opposite meaning.

Binyella, m, Mub
Armed with a dagger, he is prepared for war. This name alludes to someone well-equipped to confront his adversaries. The meaning could also be stretched to refer to someone ready to face any challenge.

Binyugha, m, Mub
Literally, if he loosens it, it won't be fruitful. This refers to a matter that should not be tampered with.

Bisangha, m/f, Mub
All is well and good. Dialogue has prevailed and calm has been restored. It could also refer to a state of goodwill or well-being.

Bitebba, m, Mub
The home is now calm or peaceful. Stability has been restored to the home or family. This also refers to a child who brings about this.

Bitnyong(a), m, Mub
The home or village has issues to settle. A child born during a period of challenge may also be given this name.

Biyella, m, Mub
The village is in a state of crisis. This is a common name for male children born during the period of a king's death.

Bobba, m, Mub
An issue that is lost or missing.

Bobbilla, m/f Mub
The village has been regained or reborn. A state of recovery and renewal in the village has been established or regained.

Bobdinga, m, Mub
The village insignia or spear is missing. He has lost his spear.

Bobga, m, Mub
Kinship cannot be lost.

Bobgala, m, Mub
The exact meaning of this name hasn't been ascertained. However, it is a common name for a male child whose parents had difficulty in conceiving a child.

Bobigha, m, Mub
I have not regained the village.

Bobmia, m/f, Mub
Face to face with an issue. This refers to an issue that besets one.

A Dictionary of Popular Bali Names

Bobyekgha, m, Mub
He has found an empty land. He has discovered new land.

Bobnyongha, m, Mub
He has retrieved lost matters. He has rediscovered past issues of importance.

Bobvalla, m, Mub
He has confronted death.

Bobyek, m/f, Mub
I have met an empty compound.

Bobyigha, m/f, Mub
He has made my once empty compound fruitful again. He has brought back life and happiness to my homestead.

Bochangkō, m, Mug
What are they proud of? What accounts for their pride?

Boghukō, m, Mug
What is the object of their jealousy?

Boghuma, f, Mug
I have been ambushed.

Boghumtang, m, Mug
They have met and plotted.

Bohbimwō, m/f, Mug
Who can be trusted?

Bohbongmeh, m/f, Mug
Not everyone is good.

Bohmbad, f, Mug
The exact meaning is yet to be established. The name is commonly given to a female child born after many have died and scepticism about her survival is entertained.

Bohkokō, f, Mug
Why are they hunting for me? Why are they after me? What do they want to take?

Bohtaakō, f, Mug
What do they want?

Bokamamdzem, m/f, Mug
A lot is still unknown.

Bokuna, f, Mub
You have lost a sibling.

Bolla, f, Mub
Egg, kinship.

Bommun, f, Mug
One's personality.

33

Bong, m/f, Mug
Goodness, kindness, grace.

Bongam, m, Mug
A good story, good news.

Bongbedla, m/f, Mug
What am I hoping for? I've been deprived of all goodness. I am currently deprived. I am yet to experience kindness.

Bongkumi, m/f, Mug
All that glitters is not gold.

Bongmun, m/f, Mug
This means a good person; one who exhibits kindness.

Bongnyikob, m/f, Mug
This refers to God's goodness; divine favour.

Bosilla, f, Mub
This means pride. This is also a wedding name that means pleasure time.

Bosungkō, f, Mug
What are they saying? What have they stated?

Bosunglan, f, Mug
Let them say it clearly. Let it be explained properly.

Bosungmeh, f, Mug
Let them say everything.

Botambuh, m, Mug
Evil or harm done to an innocent person.

Bowla, m/f, Mub
This means kinship, that is, family conntectedness.

Bovikō, f, Mug
No one knows the hearts of his/her children. A child's heart or personality is not predictable.

Bubbilla, m, Mub
The village is has been lost or defeated. See Bobbilla for an opposite meaning.

Bulla, m, Mub
This means suffering; that is, a state of affliction. Such a name speaks to the conditions of the parents at the time of the child's naming. It is also probable that a child could be named thus if he is in a state of affliction or ill-health during the naming ceremony.

Buma, m, Mub
This is a name given to a child born during wartime.

Bumbedgha, m, Mub
War has ended. This is a name given to mark the end of a feud between two or more parties.

Bumkubong, m, Mug
Literally, this means a weak and sickly person.

Bumlaa, m, Mub
This means to spark off war.

Bumlangmia, m, Mub
I am surrounded by enemies, war or difficulties.

Bumsadmia, m, Mub
War has spared me.

Bungha, m, Mub
He is hard like a stone. He is an all weather person. This name is often given to a child expected to overcome challenges in life.

C

Chahmuchang, m, Mug
This name refers to one who pretends to sympathize with someone's misfortune but secretly delighted at such a condition.

Chifini, m/f, Mug
This means living temporally. It is commonly given to a child whose mother has lost several children. See Bohmbad.

Chijohfom, m. Mug
This conveys a sense of living between and betwixt enemies.

D

Debidgha, m, Mug
You can't escape from your house or family.

Debilla, m, Mub
One who runs from home.

Dahkoba, m, Mub
You can't leave your bed.

Daiga, m, Mub
The king's family is never lost.

Daikohga, m, Mub
You can't leave land or hill; you are always entangled in some way to your native soil.

Daisongha, m/f, Mub
You cannot escape/stop from good.

Damma, m, Mub
This refers to a close collaborator to the king such as a notable (nkom). It also means the first ones.

Dangmia, m/f, Mub
He or she has acquired me.

Danseh, m, Mub
He is not selfish.

Danyebba, m/b, Mub
He or she has acquired property or land.

Dayebga, m, Mub
You can't leave your father's land or birth place. Also see Daikogha.

Dehgha, m, Mub
This means a hole or pit. Metaphorically, it means the one who keeps my secrets safe from others.

Dehse, m/f, Mub
He or she cannot be measured. It also means his/her personality is beyond measure.

Dehvalla (Dehva), m, Mub
You are invoking death.

Dema, m, Mub
It simply means immunity. This refers to someone who has immunity.

Denseh, m, Mub
There is no one to rely on. No one can be trusted entirely.

Dimia, m, Mub
You have plotted against me.

Dimma, m, Mub
He has come back to life. This name has resonance with elementary beliefs in reincarnation. See similar names like Babila, Nahbila etc.

Dingha, m, Mub
Spear. This refers to a son who has proved my manhood. It is also commonly spelt as Dinga.

Dingana, m, Mub
An insignia; that is, a spear with medicine.

Dingbella, m, Mub
The poison is finished.

Dingbobga, m, Mub
The spear will not be missing. A spear shot can't be totally lost, it must bring back something.

Dingbulla, m, Mub
This means a long flat spear. The name is also borne by the holder of a traditional insignia.

Dingka'a, m, Mub
I now have enough spears. Figuratively, it means I now have enough sons.

Dingsangha, m, Mub
This simply means a suitable spear.

Dobdingha, m, Mub
I have pinned my spear into the earth. That is, I am sure of my succession. I am now sure that someone (a son) will succeed me upon my death.

Dobgangha, m, Mub
I have planted my roots. It also means you are the mat of my fence; that is, the one to adorn my home.

Dobgima, m, Mub
I have pinned my fig tree. A live tree planted for a new compound. This name is often given to a designated successor.

Dobla, m, Mub
It has reached a fixed or secured state. This describes a state of normalcy or stability.

Dobli, m, Mub
The family's seed has been planted.

Dohbilla, m, Mub
Grandfather has returned or been reborn.

Dohkea, m, Mub
Grandfather has grown up.

Dohsang, m, Mub
Grandfather has been met.

Dohvalla, m, Mub
The grandfather of death.

Dohvoma, m, Mub
The grandfather of the Voma cult; or it could simply mean Voma's grandfather

Donko, m, Mug
What have I begged for?

Dugga, m, Mub
Something that is non-flammable; something immune to fire.

Dumia, m, Mub
He has scolded or rebuked me. It also possibly means he has scolded me and therefore brought me back to consciousness.

Duna, m, Mub
Leg. He will be able to do everything when he grows up.

Dzebong, m, Mug
One who does kind things. It also means a kind-hearted person.

Dzika, m/f, Mug
Thanks, gratitude.

F

Fakgha, m, Mub
This refers to someone who is careless and unconcerned.

Feh, m/f, Mub
This is a common name given to a follower of a set of twins.

Fobua, m, Mub
Fresh tree leaves.

Fofung, m, Mug
This is a name given to a child born on Dzimbufung.

Fogha, m, Mub
Grass or weed. It also means a gift from the bush.

Fokenmun, m, Mug
Literally, it means king of youths. This name also means a young promising fellow.

Foliba, m, Mug
This means master or king of the sea.

Fombutu, m, Mug
This is the name given to a child born on Ntanmbutu.

Fomungwi, f, Mug
Queen. A woman installed with the king.

Foncham, m, Mug
This tends to be given to a child born on Foncham, the customary day of rest.

Fongo, m, Mug
This tends to be given to a child born on Ngo.

Fongu, m, Mug
Like the preceding name, this tends to be given to a child born on Ngo.

Fongwen, m, Mug
This tends to be given to a child born on Ntungwen or at the farm. The farm symbolises an area of primary economic activity so this could be applied to any site of modern economic activity.

Fongwi, f, Mug
A woman installed with the man succeeding.

Fuhchiyah, m, Mug
Where shall I keep my treasure?

Fuhya, m, Mug
Where is the treasure?

Fuhdzem, m, Mug
A treasure one never thought of; that is a child born when the mother was no longer certain of her reproductive capacity.

Fuhkudju, m, Mug
One who does not enjoy the benefits of one's treasure.

Fuhmun, m, Mug
Literally, this means someone's treasure.

Fuhndambab, m, Mug
A child born after several have died and whose survival is uncertain.

Fuhngwah, m, Mug
This means a lost treasure.

G

Gaba, m, Mub,
I know it.

Gabana, m, Mub
This refers to the king's favourite wine. It is also a royal title.

Gabba, m, Mub
Separated or isolated

Gabella, m, Mub
The kingship has ended. You have disrespected constituted authority.

Gabga, m, Mub
Who knows tomorrow?

Gabgha, m/f, Mub
This refers to something that cannot be shared or divided.

Gabilla, m, Mub
The King has returned or been reborn. This name tends to be given to male children born after the passing away of a king.

Gabsa, m, Mub
He has no lovers.

Gabsaga, m, Mub
He doesn't know who his lovers are.

Gabsagha, m, Mub
One never knows where one will be buried.

Gabseh, m, Mub
I don't know.

Gabsia, m, Mub
I know myself. Know yourself.

Gabsonga, m, Mub
He does not value what has been done to him.

Gabuma, m, Mub
This means the king's war; that is, one declared by him.

Gabvase, m, Mub
He does not know death. Death is foreign to him.

A Dictionary of Popular Bali Names

Gadinga, m, Mub
This means the king's spear.

Gaduna, m, Mub
The king's feet. See Duna.

Gakeh, m/f, Mub
The king has ruled it.

Gakehmi (a), m, Mub
The king has freed me from difficulties.

Gakidla, f, Mub
The king's sleeping mat. Figuratively, this means the king's beloved or favourite wife.

Galaa, m, Mub
This means the king's fire.

Galabe, m, Mub
Literally, this means fire or star. It is also a title which means king

Galanga, m, Mub
A royal title reserved exclusively for kings.

Galega, m, Mub
He is from within the house. It is also a royal title.

Gami, m, Mub
You have pushed me.

Gamgha, m/f, Mub
It is a matter that can't be talked about.

Gamseh, m, Mub
He is not rejecting the secret.

Gamnyamgha, f, Mub
You can't predict when it will happen.

Gamua, m, Mub
He is tired of talking.

Gana, m, Mub
Literally, this means medicine, chieftaincy or kingship.

Gang, m, Mub
This means a boundary, fence.

Gangbobga, m, Mub
My boundary will not be lost.

Gangdia, m, Mub
My fig tree has taken roots. It also means my boundary has been established.

Gangmi(a), m, Mub
You have plotted against me.

Gangtebba, m, Mub
A boundary dispute has been settled peacefully.

Gangtihbobga, m, Mub
The fig tree pinned here can't wither.

Ganseh, m, Mub
A family ran so smoothly that it does not need medicine to prevent problems.

Ganwana, m, Mub
The king's representative to the Nwanas.

Ganyam, m, Mub
This refers to the king's durables.

Ganyonga, m, Mub
This is a royal title. It also means challenges or problems.

Gasadla, m, Mub
Royalty or kingly status fits him.

Gasuh, m, Mub
This means the chief or master of the moon.

Gavadsen, m, Mub
There is no medicine to prevent death.

Gawabilla (Gawabit), m, Mub
I am gathering the king's spears.

Gehyeck, m, Mub
Visit an abandoned home or family.

Gennah, m, Mub
He has matured or developed.

Gima, m, Mub
Literally, this means a fig tree. It also means I have settled well.

Ginna, m, Mub
I have worsened my problems.

Gua, m, Mub
Leopard

Guka'a, m, Mub
The mouth talks a lot.

Gurb, m, Mub
To aim at something.

Gurbdinga, m, Mub
I have aimed with a spear and have succeeded.

Gurbvalla, m, Mub
Death is eyeing you but you can't escape.

Gurdmia, m, Mub
Rejoice with me.

Gurkudla, f, Mub
Leopard's skin. This is also a wedding name which means the one who will give me a good name.

Gurmua, m, Mub
The leopard is tired.

Guryigha, m, Mub
A leopard's head; a small leopard in the house.

Gusasiya, m, Mub
Gossips have torn us apart.

Gushua, m, Mub
The mouth has redeemed me.

Gusi, f, Mub
Arm yourself properly before the unexpected happens.

Gusonga, m, Mub
A bad turn received for a good one.

Guyenyonga, m, Mub
The mouth mars a lot of things.

Inyakō, m/f, Mug
What is he/she proud of?

Imunmboi, m/f, Mug
Everyone has problems.

J

Jabosung, f, Mug
Let them tell.

Jalla, m/f, Mub
Figurative - insects have burst the calabash. The secret has been revealed. This also refers to a woman who has raised one's prestige.

Jamvalla, m, Mub
You have delivered your death, i.e. a child who will kill you or will die.

Janga, m, Mub
You can't shake me.

Jangha, m, Mub
Promised. A promised one.

Jangman, m, Mug
Self-pride.

Jangmia, m/f, Mub
He/she has promised a deal with me.

Janvagha, m, Mub
You are feeding death or your enemies.

Jella, m, Mub
This means to hush up a matter.

Jenka'a, m/f, Mub
Enmity is widespread in this world. It also means my enemies are many.

Jenmia, m/f, Mub
People envy me when I have nothing.

Jenna, m, Mub
I have been deceived.

Jijeb, m, Mub
I am wasting my time with an issue of little or no value.

Jinga, m, Mub
Determination. I am determined.

Jomi(a), m/f, Mub
She/he has told me a lie. He/she has deceived me.

Jongha, f, Mub
Thorns of the palm fronds.

Jubsia, f, Mub
You are anxious over nothing.

Jugha, m, Mub
One who does not want to be smeared with filth.

K

Kah, f, Mug
Grandmother.

Kabisen, f, Mub
I have nothing more to say because it is above me.

Kabsah, f, Mug
Refers to a bride price paid in court on account of a dispute.

Kadmia, m/f, Mub
I have been ambushed.

Kahkuna, m/f, Mub
Family circles.

Kahngho, f, Mug
This name tended to be given to a child who was believed to have died and returned by means of reincarnation.

Kahyeba, f, Mub
I have bought the land. I have acquired my own space.

Kangha, m, Mub
I'm now clever or wise. I'm matured.

Kangmia, m, Mub
You are in doubt about me.

Kapsalla, m, Mub
He has gathered dirt and thrown away.

Kayeba, m, Mub
Literally, this means grandmother earth. This metaphorically refers to someone with a strong determination.

Kehbila, m, Mub
He has taken back the lineage. Such a name alludes to a man that has successfully regained his lineage.

Kehbuma, m, Mub
I have succeeded despite the disagreement or challenges in my marriage. I have emerged victorious from the war.

Kehdinga, m, Mub
I have taken the spear.

Kehfun, m, Mub
Literally, it means a key. This name is also given to one who has brought prosperity to his family or born when disappointments and failures have been cleared off.

Kehgana, m, Mub
I have taken medicine. Such a name is suitable for a child whose parents obtained fertility treatment prior to conception.

Kehkuna, m, Mub
I have taken back a brother. This generally refers to actions that have saved one's family from a challenge or problem.

Kehkungha, f, Mub
You can save the family.

Kehla, m/f, Mub
You have inherited challenges.

Kehmia, f, Mub
She has freed me from trouble.

Kehmina, m, Mub
I have received camwood.

Kehnyonga, m/f, Mub
She has resolved the problems.

Kehsap, f, Mub
I've wasted my time on something that won't be of profit to me.

Kehsigha, f, Mub
I have received and kept.

Kehvagha, m, Mub
You cannot take someone's death.

Kehwalla, f, Mub
She has taken over possession of the compound. This name is commonly given to the daughter of a beloved wife (particularly in a polygamous marriage).

Kehyeb(a), f, Mub
She has acquired the land whereby land serves as a metaphor for children.

Kenna, f, Mub
Pride.

Kennyikob, m/f, Mug
God's gift or favour

Kibobga, f, Mub
I hardly forget what I hear.

Kidla (Killa), f, Mub
Mat; the mat of my bed.

Kigha, m/f, Mub
It can't be taken.

Kijita, m, Mub
This is a common name for a male child born after the death of his father. Its exact meaning is unknown.

Kingtua, m/f, Mug
I'm trying to save my life.

Kivalla, m, Mub
I have heard and suffered for it.

Kodmia, m, Mub
I have been caught red-handed.

Kohbangmia, m, Mub
The hill has defeated me.

Kohga, m, Mub
Not easily catchable. Something that is difficult to track or trap.

Kohkunga, f, Mub
Firewood that is non flammable.

Kohla, m, Mub
Literally, this means a hill; here, hill symbolises challenges, problems or ill-luck. Consequently, the name also refers to one's problems or ill-fortune.

Kohlaga, m, Mub
It can't catch fire. This item or device is non-flammable.

Kohyidla, m, Mub
A hill top.

Kona, m, Mub
Family or brotherly matter.

Kongninyikob, m, Mug
God's love.

Kosen, m, Mub
I have not caught anything.

Kosidumi, m, Mub
A slave has abused me.

Koyela (Kwoyila), m/f, Mub
Save your life. This tends to be given to a child born through difficulties.

Kudbilla, m, Mub
I'm developing the village.

Kudchambi, m, Mub
Proverbial; remove the beam from your eye and then you will see the speck in your friend's eye.

Kudkuju, m, Mug
One who never enjoys one's labour.

Kudlegha, f, Mub
Build the house.

Kudnyonga, f, Mub
It is because of family issues.

Kumbega, m, Mub
Brotherliness can never end. There is no end to brotherliness.

Kumbella, m, Mub
The lineage has ended or become extinct.

Kumunsen, m, Mub
You have not forgotten her.

Kuna, f, Mub
Pertains to family and kinship.

Kunbanmia, m, Mub
This labour is above me.

Kunbedga, m, Mub
Brotherhood is endless. Also see Kumbega above.

Kunbuma, m, Mub
This refers to associates of war. It is also interpreted to mean one's death bed. Others have also interpreted the name to mean internecine strife.

Kungaba, m, Mub
Brotherliness tends to be ruined by unfortunate situations.

Kungha, f, Mub
It must be identified.

Kunjemia, f, Mub
My brothers dislike me.

Kunjuma, m, Mub
Brotherhood is desirable.

Kunlemia, f, Mub
My brothers have abandoned me.

Kunlemuga, f, Mub
She has laboured and left me alone. Such a name tends to be given to a female child whose mother dies just after giving birth.

A Dictionary of Popular Bali Names

Kunseh, f, Mub
This name pertains to someone without a uterine (i.e. from the same womb) brother or sister.

Kunsonaa, m/f, Mub
Kinship or family relationship is good.

Kunuwō, m/f, Mug
Is there anyone without problems?

Kunvagha, m/f, Mub
Death is recognisable.

Kunvalla, m/f, Mub
I cannot recognise death.

Kusamia, f, Mub
This is a fruitful journey.

Kusilangmia, m, Mub
I am surrounded by enemies.

Kwadkap, m, Mug
Literally, someone who is a spendthrift, an extravagant person.

L

Laah, m, Mub
Fire. Fire is a potent symbol among the Chamba. It is employed to convey diverse meanings in different social contexts.

Ladji, m, Mub
Father.

Lahfork, m/f, Mub
A hunting ground.

Lahndamun, f, Mug
This name has a proverbial meaning; it means the state of one's house is best known by one's self.

Langbaa, m, Mub
People have plotted against.

Langmia, m, Mub
I have been surrounded.

Langyeba, m, Mub
Surround the ground or territory.

Lebaga, m, Mub
Fatherhood can't be bought. It also means a son can't beget the father.

Lebga, m, Mub
God's gift. I've avoided them yet I've been identified.

Lebidgha, m, Mub
You can't abandon your village.

Lebkuna, f, Mub
I can't leave (abandon) my brothers and sisters; others have interpreted this name to mean I have delivered my brothers and sisters.

Lebkunga, f, Mub
Brotherliness cannot be bought with money.

Lebnyonga, f, Mub
I have forgotten completely about the matter.

Lebsia, f, Mub
She has freed herself.

Lebsiga, f, Mub
Proverbial, meaning one does not deliver oneself.

Lebsongha, f, Mub
You can't buy goodness from somebody.

Lebvalla, f, Mub
Buy off death.

Lebyilla, f, Mub
I have saved myself.

Legha, f, Mub
A child meant for the house or compound; that which cannot be bought.

Legima, m, Mub
I have bought my fig tree.

Lehdogha, m, Mub
The farm has ended. This could be understood in two related ways – first that one's farm no longer produces anything and secondly that one has reached the bounds of one's farms. Farm is symbolic of a range of things – family, economic productivity or generally, the tools of economic production.

Lehkuna, f, Mub
You have abandoned your brothers.

Lehkungha, f, Mub
You can't abandon your brothers.

Lehna, f, Mub
My hands are open. I am innocent. Also see Mbongho

Lehnyin(a), f, Mub
I am innocent. I am surprised at what has happened.

Lehnyonga, f, Mub
She can't wish away the matter. Keep aside the challenges and welcome the baby.

Lehvalla, m/f, Mub
Death takes away people yet more are born.

Lehyidla, m, Mub
Accept that all are good.

Lehyogha, m/f, Mub
Proverbial; you can't throw away your intestines.

Lema/Lenlagha, f, Mub
Hide my fault or weakness.

Lemah, f, Mub
It used to provide immunity.

Lemia, m, Mub
I have been neglected.

Lenna, m, Mub
My hands are clean, i.e. I am innocent. Also see Lehna.

Leoga, f, Mub
Do not throw it away.

Lesia, f, Mub
I have neglected myself.

Lesiga, m/f, Mub
This name has three meanings; leave everything to the world to judge. I can't let down myself or be careless. Blood is thicker than water.

Leyigha, f, Mub
The compound has been left to me alone.

Lih/Lihlobnikō, m/f, Mug
What else is left for the eye?

Lima, m/f, Mub
It is my day or time.

Limi, m, Mub
Something that has absorbed or engrossed me.

Lobga, m, Mub
A gift obtained from prayer which shouldn't be made fun of.

Lokunga, f, Mub
If you are better off, do not laugh at others.

Lonyonga, f, Mub
Laugh at the matter.

Lovalla, f, Mub
I have laughed at death's actions.

Luma, f, Mub
Seed; metaphorically, it refers to a starting point, the beginning. It also means, who do you resemble in your behaviour?

Lumbobga, m/f, Mub
Kinship or family relationship cannot be lost.

Lumfi, m, Mub
Literally, New Year's Day. This name is suitably, given to a child born on New Year's Day or soon thereafter.

Lumvalla, m, Mub
Death's family. This name tends to be given to a male child whose mother has lost several children prior to his birth.

M

Maankoh, f, Mub
A child followed by a set of twins. This is often an additional name given in retrospect.

Magsia, f, Mub
Nobody is the author of one's self.

Majisung, m/f, Mug
Don't reveal all that you know.

Makajia, f, Mub
There is no family without a graveyard.

Ma'ndanjo, f, Mug
Avoid the sight of something.

Ma'ndansam, f, Mug
Don't miss out.

Mantan, f, Mug
This name tends to be given to a female child born on Ntanbani.

Manyi, f, Mug
A mother of twins.

Mbebbeb, m/f, Mug
I'm only a caretaker.

Mbebwō, m/f, Mug
Whom am I waiting for?

Mbihkō, m/f, Mug
What accounts for this matter?

Mboja, m/f, Mug
Many hands do light work.

Mbongbowō, f, Mug
For whom do I look beautiful?

Mbongiwō, f, Mug
For whose good is it anyway?

Mbongo, f, Mug
My hands are open. I am innocent. Also see Lehna

Mbotiji, m/f, Mug
False accusation; I can't be forced to say what I don't know.

Mbuhmun, m/f, Mug
Literally, this means one's weakness or flaws.

Mbuhnu, m, Mug
An innocent person.

Mbungdō, f, Mug
A calm woman; a beautiful and befitting one.

Medingha, m, Mub
Fighting against a long held tradition. This refers to an advocate for change.

Mihnadzam, m/f, Mug
The last sight. One who has survived to see the world. This name tends to be given to a surviving child whose mother has buried several children.

Mohkumi, m, Mug
It never rains but it pours.

Moiwō, f, Mug
There should be no discrimination; all are the same.

Momgha, m, Mub
Not differentiated or distinguishable.

Mua, m, Mub
Hidden, concealed or veiled.

Mubuhwō, m/f, Mug
Who is on my side?

Muchiya, m, Mug
I have no hiding place for my treasure.

Muhme, f, Mub
She has refused or rejected me.

Muhnyonga, f, Mub
I'm tired of talking.

Muhvalla, m, mub
You can't be tired of grieving upon someone's death.

Muhyilla, f, Mub
I've concealed my head; i.e. I have saved my life.

Muhyo, f, Mug
I will see before I believe.

Mukahtam, f, Mub
Full of one'self while stuck. Refers to one already caught in a net with little prospects of a rescue.

Mukonghu, f, Mug
A beloved person. Someone's darling.

Mukuna, f, Mub
Is it good to disown your brother?

Mulem, f, Mug
Where shall I hide it?

Mullah, m, Mub
Also a title; a king's retainer at succession.

Mullaku, m, Mug
Death comes to all. Someday, I shall also die.

Mumia, f, Mub
I have not rejected your statement.

Munawō, m, Mug
Who is my own person? Whose support can I count on?

Munaya, m/f, Mug
Where is the one whose support I can count on? Where is my own person?

Mundung, m, Mug
No one is entirely free from problems.

Munimbomi, m/f, Mug
Each person's character is unique.

Munjibō, m/f, Mub
No one knows.

Munjikō, m/f, Mug
If I had known. Who knows?

Munse, f, Mub
Something that cannot be prevented or concealed.

Munyenbō, f, Mub
I do not care about the matter

Munyonga, f, Mub
I cannot hide from challenges.

Muvagha, m/f, Mub
I cannot prevent death.

N

Nadinga, f, Mub
I trample on spears.

Nahbila, f, Mub
Mother has returned.

Nahbudla, f, Mub
A tall woman, suitably given as a wedding name.

Nahbulla, f, Mub
A child born through difficulties; this name has a masculine synonym, Koyela.

Nahbum, f, Mub
A child born during a war; this name has a masculine synonym, Buma.

Nahbungha, f, Mub
I have seen or picked up the stone. This could be interpreted as taking up a challenge with enthusiasm.

Nahdalla, f, Mub
This name is often given to the first princess born on the throne. Its exact meaning is yet to be established.

Nahgim(a) f, Mub
She has come with certainty.

Nahgwaa, f, Mub
The first of a set of female twins.

Nahjela/Nahjewa, f, Mub
The second of a set of female twins.

Nahjomia, f, Mub
She has deceived me.

Nahkum, f, Mub
This name tends to be given to the follower of a set of twins. Also see Feh. Unlike Feh which is applicable to both genders, this name is exclusive to females.

Nahkuna, f, Mub
My brother can't deceive me.

Nahkupid, f, Mug
This name tends to be given to a child born on the day the Kupid dance is performed at the palace.

Nahlegha, f, Mub
A child born in the house.

Nahlesu, f, Mub
A child born in the farm; one regarded as a gift from the farm.

Nahlim, f, Mub
Mother of the day.

Nahnwana, f, Mub
A child born during the Voma festival or on the day a member of the Nwana is being initiated

Nahnyama, f, Mub
A durable mineral. This refers to someone or something trustworthy and enduring.

Nahnyeni (fili), f, Mub
The third of a set of female triplets.

Nahnyonga, f, Mub
A popular name that tends to be given to a female child born at the succession of a new king.

Nahnyuma, f, Mub
A beautiful woman who makes me happy. This name is also a popular wedding name.

Nahpagha, f, Mub
She cannot be otherwise.

Nahsadla, f, Mub
A good befitting woman; also suitable as a wedding name.

Nahsang, f, Mub
A child born under a lucky star. It also simply means lucky star.

Nahseh, f, Mub
She is yet to mature. This name conveys hope for a prosperous future.

Nahsima, f, Mub
Mother has been reborn. Also see Nahbila.

Nahsona, f, Mub
This name tends to be given to a female child born in the month of Gwansoa.

Nahtuh, f, Mub
This name is often given to a child born on the day that the king has a special gathering at ntuh.

Nahsua, f, Mub
This alludes to a female child born in the month of Sonia.

Nahvalla, f, Mub
Our family is certain about death.

Nahvoma, f, Mub
This is a popular name for a female child born in the month of Vomsoa or during the voma festival.

Nehwalla, f, Mub
The mother or matriarch of the family.

Nahwedga, f, Mub
Proverbial; hang your bag where you will take it. Keep within your limits. It also means cut your coat according to your size.

Nahwolla, f, Mub
You have crossed the bridge (water). This refers to one who has overcome a challenge or obstacle.

Nahwubba, f, Mub
Mother has returned. Also see Nahbila and Nahsima.

Nahyella, f, Mub
Refers to a light complexioned woman often given as a wedding name.

Nasiga, f, Mub
She belongs to the old compound.

Nchamukong, m, Mub
As prosperous as black jack.

Nchokobmundzih, m, Mug
Proverb; there can be no witness for anything done alone.

Nchombōwō, m/f, Mug
I am not free from anyone.

Nchonu, m/f, Mug
I have involved myself greatly.

Nchuhnu, m/f, Mug
The day an issue will be addressed.

Nchungong, m, Mug
One who saves the village or home.

Nchuyekō, f, Mug
What is the mouth doing?

Ndadzam, m, Mug
No one knows what is in a dark room. A dark room is always full of surprises.

Ndahnjo, m, Mug
I will see.

A Dictionary of Popular Bali Names

Ndamnted, f, Mug
Potentially a lucky charm. Fruitful marriage in the palace or polygamous family depends on luck. This is often given as a wedding name.

Ndango, m, Mug
A child born on Ngo.

Ndasi, m, Mug
A child born on Ndansi.

Ndawokamnu, f, Mug
Whose house is without problems or challenges?

Ndaya, m, Mug
Where shall I pass? How will I go through?

Ndibabongha, m/f, Mug
Literally means good times; when the going is good. It refers to the fact that people rejoice in good times.

Ndibibō, m, Mug
Before it was time.

Ndibmun, m/f, Mug
There is a time for everything. Each person has an opportunity.

Ndibnyikob, m/f, Mug
God's time is the best.

Ndipnu, m/f, Mug
Refers to a time when something is expected to occur.

Ndungbōwō, f, Mug
From whom am I free?

Ndzambad, m, Mug
The last straw that breaks the camel's back.

Ndzammawoe, m/f, Mug
Who are my supporters?

Ndzamnu, m, Mug
The last thing that matters; a cornerstone.

Ndzika, m/f, Mug
Thanks.

Ndzombombom, m, Mug
Prayers tend to differ from person to person.

Ndzomkō, m, Mug
What is prayer?

Ndzongsona, Mub
A peaceful place or atmosphere.

Nebensen, m, Mub
No one takes sides with me.

Ngamchaa, m/f, Mug
I've been silenced by the house.

Ngehdab, m/f, Mug
A child who adores the house. One who loves being indoors.

Ngedtikō, m/f, Mug
A child who likes the house. See Ngehdab above.

Ngidduwō, m, Mug
Be careful with those you deal.

Ngongho, m, Mug
A jealous home.

Ngongmun, m, Mug
One's home.

Ngwahmbō, m/f, Mug
I do not know my guilt because I am open-minded with everyone.

Nihmia, f, Mub
The problem is above me.

Nina, f, Mug
First female child in a family.

Ninantan, f, Mug
A female child born on Ntanbani.

Ningmua, m, Mub
What am I to you? I'm widely known.

Ninyongha, f, Mub
The matter has been concealed.

Njankadji, m, Mug
One who always complains of hunger.

Njekō, m/f, Mug
What am I doing when others have made progress?

Nji, m, Mug
Title and prefix - given to Mfontes (Sub-chiefs) and reputable Nchinteds (palace retainers); derived from Bamum.

Njijekō, m, Mug
If I knew, what would I do?

Njinuwō, m, Mug
Who knows everything?

Njongndab, m, Mug
A plot within the house can't fail. Proverbial.

Nkakanu, m, Mug
A perpetual matter.

Nkakō, m, Mug
What am I again?

A Dictionary of Popular Bali Names

Nkambem, m Mub
Leader of a group or organisation.

Nkoeti, m, Mug
A fraternal deputy to a successor.

Nkohtan, f, Mug
A child born on Nkohntan.

Nkom, m, Mug
Title; the king's councillor; a noble man. See introductory notes on Nkom.

Nkuhti, m, Mug
Nothing can be added to what I already have. A child got out of wedlock and brought to the family.

Nogbanmia, m, Mub
The world has amazed me.

Nogha, m, Mub
He is blind to truth.

Nsonseh, m, Mub
Good deeds are few.

Ntseya, m/f, Mug
Where have I reached?

Ntinuwō, m/f, Mug
Whose problem have I met (solved)?

Ntumvi, m, Mug
A message to the world.

Ntungwen, m, Mug
A child born on Ntungwen.

Nua(h), m, Mub
Eye.

Nubia, m, Mub
My eyes have seen this day.

Nubidla, m, Mub
He has gone and returned.

Nubitgha, m, Mub
I cannot leave my village because of enmity. Leave everything in God's hands.

Nubila, m, Mub
I cannot escape my father's land or run away from home.

Nubo, m, Mug
It is their matter, not mine.

Nubokō, m, Mug
What sort of matter cannot be solved?

Nubong, m/f, Mug
A pleasant matter.

Nubonsi, f, Mug
The earth decides all cases because it receives all sorts of corpses.

Nubowŏ, m/f, Mug
Who is responsible for this matter?

Nuga, m, Mub
Nothing pains me.

Nugangha, m, Mug
Challenges meant for me.

Nuilla, m, Mub
Run to safety. Try to save your life.

Nuitum, f, Mug
A concealed secret is best known only to the heart.

Nujam, m, Mub
It never rains but it pours. Also see Mohkumi.

Nukamndawŏ, m/f, Mub
There is no house without challenges.

Nukandzem, m, Mug
There are more challenges yet to be faced

Nukamya, m, Mug
There is no society without its challenges or difficulties.

Nukuna, m, Mub
My brothers and sisters' eyes are watching me. It also means one should avoid wicked relatives.

Nukungha, m, Mub
One can't completely avoid one's family.

Nulla(h), m, Mub
As sweet as honey.

Numbumma, m/f, Mug
My own personal challenges.

Numibŏ, m, Mug,
Troubleshooting is endless.

Numun, m, Mug
Your problems are left to you.

Numvi, m, Mug
Earthly matters.

Nundabndab, m, Mug
Every home has its problems.

Nundo'ya, f, Mug
Where do problems come from?

Nuninchu, m, Mug
Everyday has its challenges.

Nulagha, m, Mub
You cannot run from fire whereby fire stands for challenges. Hence the name also means no one can run away from challenges.

Nuntua, f, Mug
I am the only person who knows what is in my heart or what makes me happy.

Nunyonga, f, Mub
Stay out of trouble.

Nusen, m, Mub
He has not escaped.

Nutoto, m, Mug
One's troubles keep piling. It never rains but it pours.

Nuvagha, m, Mub
No one can escape from death. A clear reminder of every human being's fate.

Nuvalla, m, Mub
Run away from death.

Nuvi, m, Mub
The woes of childbirth.

Nuyebga, m, Mub
You can't run away from the world.

Nuyilla, m, Mub
Save yourself; escape with your head.

Nwana, m, Mub
Rain, peacemaker, i.e. the consecrated one. Also granted as a title; Also given to male children born during the Voma festival or in the month of Vomsoa.

Nwanyam, m, Mub
Wait for the time or sun.

Nwanyechgha, m, Mub
One who keeps watch over a grave in an empty compound.

Nwayigha, m, Mub
I am waiting for a grave; this name tends to be given to a child born into a childless family due to high infant mortality rates.

Nyahngang, m, Mub
The boundary has been mixed up.

Nyakuna, f, Mub
I have encountered brotherliness.

Nyagassa, m, Mub
I have mixed up the kingship.

Nyalla, f, Mub
Wind, breeze. Something refreshing.

Nyaluma, f, Mub
Family entanglement; refers to a child got out of wedlock and brought into the family.

Nyam, m, Mug
Meat, beef, flesh.

Nyama, m, Mub
The sun.

Nyamchah/Nyamosi, m, Mug
Earthly meat.

Nyamgamsen, m, Mub
The sun does not recognise anybody. In other words, the sun does not discriminate against any individual.

Nyamkimah, m, Mug
This refers to an animal that cannot be domesticated or reared. The name tended to be given to a child whose chances of survival was seriously doubted, particularly in a context where other infants had died.

Nyamkingangmi, m, Mug
This refers to a neckless animal; a person without a network of supporters. This name speaks to the context surrounding the birth of its bearer. It is probable that the young parents had been abandoned or ignored during the period of the child's birth, which is generally at odds with local ideology.

Nyamndon, m, Mug
This refers to a problem-ridden animal; an animal that begets ill-luck. This name tends to be given to a male child born during a period of grave misfortune in the family. Again, this resonates with the idea of names as a marker of a people's history.

Nyamsangha, m, Mub
What was long-awaited has come to pass or materialised.

Nyanga, m, Mug
Pride.

A Dictionary of Popular Bali Names

Nyassa, m, Mub
The dirt has been mixed up.

Nyema, f, Mub
I've begged. The secret has been leaked.

Nyemkuna, f, Mub
I can't beg for or borrow a brother.

Nyonga, m/f, Mub
A problem, difficulty or challenge.

Nyongapsen, m, Mub
What else can I say? Let it be.

Nyongbadmia, m, Mub
I am overwhelmed by challenges.

Nyongbedga, m, Mub
This refers to matters too difficult to resolve.

Nyongbedla, m, Mub
Everything is finished.

Nyongbobmuga, m, Mub
The village does not suit me.

Nyongduga, f, Mub
A dormant matter.

Nyongka'a, m/f, Mub
This is a name given in a context where the parents or a family member is going through a lot of difficulties.

Nyongkwan, f, Mub
No problem.

Nyonglema, f, Mub
I'm immune to problems; old problems.

Nyonglemuga, f, Mub
Nothing hurts me; let them laugh at me as they wish.

Nyongpua, f, Mub
Something new has come.

Nyongsangha, f, Mub
Life or the world is alright.

Nyongsongha, m/f, Mub
Things can hardly be good.

Nyongsonna, f, Mub
Things are good.

Nyongtema, f, Mub
Every good thought comes from the heart.

Nyongvodla, f, Mub
There is no more trouble. The matter was peacefully resolved.

Nyuga, m, Mub
Nothing pains me; it is not small.

Nyummun, m, Mug
A thing that belongs to someone else.

Nyuyidla, m, Mub
I am gravely disliked.

Odla, f, Mub
You have admired yourself.

Odmi, f, Mub
She brings about things as if she were family.

Odmia, f, Mub
They envy me.

Odvalla, f, Mub
She admires death.

P

Padyen, m, Mub
Change one's head. This could also mean - to change one's mind.

Pagbum, m, Mub
You have borne the difficulties.

Pagpia, m, Mub
I've carried something too heavy for me.

Pagwulla, f, Mub
To carry water.

Pagyebga, m, Mub
I can't take the earth/world along with me when I die.

Pahbungha, m, Mub
Literally, it means he has carried a stone; that is, he bears a heavy load. Possibly refers to someone who bears or is expected to bear a heavy responsibility in life.

Paidingha, m, Mub
He has pinned his spears.

Paiyidla, m/f, Mub
I have given in my head; that is, I have committed myself to a particular cause.

Pakdingha, m, Mub
He has carried the spears.

Panseh, m, Mub
Reincarnated; that is, a male child who resembles a deceased relative.

Panvah, m, Mub
One who tames death. This name seems to convey the parents' hope for the newborn – precisely that he would not fall prey to an early death.

Panyena, m, Mub
We have involved or committed ourselves. This name describes the parents/family's condition at the time of the birth of the newborn. It could also be understood as a statement of commitment and willingness to bear responsibility for the life and welfare of the newborn.

A Dictionary of Popular Bali Names

Pasigha, f, Mub
Someone who does not seek recognition forcefully.

Pattem, m, Mub
It has comforted me. This refers to a child or an issue that has brought tremendous comfort, possibly to the family or parents.

Pedfork, m, Mub
Literally, it means to open up a grassy path. Simply put, it means to open the way. This conveys the parents' or family's aspiration for the newborn where the child is expected to embody the family's hope as a pathfinder.

Pedkuna, f, Mub
One who keeps one's relatives apart. The context in which such a name is chosen could be ambiguous. Probably, this name speaks to a context in which the family is divided at the time of the child's birth.

Pedkungha, m, Mub
Family love can't be divided.

Pedmia, m, Mub
You can't split the finger. Possibly, it means one is not expected to accomplish the impossible.

Pehtemma, f, Mub
Wedding name; divided thoughts. It also means she has broken my heart with her beauty.

Pengha, f, Mub
One's back. Possibly means a source of support, pillar or prop.

Penkwangha, f, Mub
You have changed your road, path or plan.

Penn, f, Mub
Describes a changed condition or person; changed

Pensia, f, Mub
You have changed.

Pensigha, m, Mub
You cannot change or transform your body or behaviour.

Penvaga, m, Mub
You can't exchange death with something else.

Penvalla, m/f, Mub
You can change death.

Penyebga, m, Mub
You cannot change the world.

Pidla, m/f, Mub
It is your problem, responsibility.

Pihga, m, Mub
I cannot give.

Pivadga, m, Mub
I cannot give in to death.

Pivagha, m, Mub
You cannot cause death to occur.

Pobmi, m, Mub
He has hypnotised me.

S

Sabum, (Sabuma), m, Mub
Literally, it means I have sought the war that is now upon me. In other words, it means I am the source of the problems or challenges I face.

Sadmia, f, Mub
A woman who is befitting to her husband. This is also a common wedding name.

Sadnyonga, f, Mub
I sought for this challenge. This is also employed as a wedding name.

Sagha, f, Mub
There is no point to search for what is clearly lost; don't cry over spilt milk.

Sahmi, f, Mug
The case is closed.

Sahnyonga, f, Mub
One who looks for a challenge.

Saila, m, Mub
Try to save yourself.

Sakumi, f, Mug
A protracted matter. This name tends to be given to a female child born when her parents have an unresolved matter.

Sakuma, m/f, Mub
One who looks for his/her relatives.

Salla, m/f, Mub
Biological reference to sex; this also means friend.

Sama, m, Mub
The male of a set of twins of opposite sexes. This name could also be awarded as a title to a man who has carried certain rites. See introductory notes on Sama.

Sambila, m, Mub
Sama has been reincarnated.

Sambum, m, Mub
The sorrows brought about by death or war.

Samdalla, m, Mub
First male child born to a new king.

Samgana, m, Mub
Medicine or drug reserved for the Samas.

Samgwa'a, m, Mub
The first of a set of male twins.

Samjela, Samjewa, m, Mub
The second of a set of male twins.

Samkea, Tafili, m, Mub
The third of a set of male triplets.

Sankusenna, m, Mub
A Sama with no relatives.
Sanmuvadga, m, Mub
One who is not afraid of death.

Sanmugala, m, Mub
A Sama who respects the king.

Sang, f, Mug
Star; lucky star.

Sangni, f, Mug
Happiness; jubilation.

Sapamaa, m, Mub
He has landed me into trouble.

Saplah, m, Mub
To light a fire. To energise a certain matter or situation.

Savalla, m, Mub
He has sought his own death.

Sayid, m/f, Mub
What I did has caused problems.

Sega, m, Mub
I will believe even without any reason.

Sehdogha, m, Mub
You cannot recall past events.

Sehnyonga, f, Mub
Think of a solution to the matter.

Sema, m, Mub
I don't worry about anything.

Semgagha, m, Mub
You can't ignore the king.

Semgha, m, Mub
I don't care about the quantity.

Semia, f, Mub
I have remembered and it hurts.

Semkuna, f, Mub
One who ignores one's brother or sister.

Semmah, f, Mub
She feels guilty.

Semmia, f, Mub
You ignore me.

Semnyonga, f, Mub
I ignore problems; one who despises all things.

Semvagha, m, Mub
You cannot ignore death.

Sibedwō, m, Mug
The earth never rejects anyone.

Sibonu, m/f, Mug
Literally, this means the finger that is at the root of the problems. The root cause of a problem or dispute.

Sigalla, m, Mub
Legs; in good health, one tends to forget about the future.

Singmia, f, Mub
I have stayed on because of this birth.

Sobilla, f, Mub
A new moon has come. This could mean a sign of hope.

Sodza, m, Mub
A child born in the month of Sodza

Sombella, m, Mub
Friendship has ended.

Sonbedmia, Sonbella, m, Mub
Goodness/kindness has come to an end.

Sonbebga, m, Mub
Goodness cannot be lost.

Songnyongha, m/f, Mub
Good for other things.

Sonnah, f, Mub
It is very good, pleasant, enjoyable or interesting.

Sonvalla, m, Mub
Death is better.

Suunyin, m, Mug
Refers to a concerted matter, truthfulness, harmonious agreement, and concord.

T

Tafry, m/f Mub
The follower of a set of twins irrespective of sex. Also see Feh.

Tamjo, m, Mug
A fruit that will bring problems. Something that will bring forth challenges.

TaNdangu, m, Mug
This is a title; it generally refers to the leader of the Ngumba cult.

Tangwi, f, Mug
Aunt; refers to father's sister or in a more generic sense, a female paternal relative.

Tankoh, m, Mub
Predecessor of a set of twins; could be given as an additional name.

Tanyi, m, Mug
This means a father of twins. See Manyi.

Tanu, m, Mug
This means a father capable of handling problems or challenges. Someone equipped with the means to deal with challenges.

Temma, f, Mub
Wedding name; my heart; where I'll pay great attention, lovable.

Tessi, m, Mub
Proverbial; even though tree leaves may age and fall off, the trees still remain upright.

Tihmia, f, Mub
I have been put aside; push me.

Tikuna, f, Mub
Do not push your relative into trouble.

Tita, m, Mub
A prince; a noble man. Also see introductory notes on Tita.

Todluma, f, Mub
I'm simply looking after my family.

Todmia, m, Mub
Exhaust me; I've been emptied of everything.

Tschimbebwō, m/f, Mug
Who am I waiting for?

Tscheya, m/f, Mug
Where have I arrived?

Tuhncha, m, Mug
A clod of soil.

Tumligha, m, Mub
I'm not sure I'll enjoy the fruits of my labour.

Tumma, m/f, Mub
I have worked and succeeded.

Tumsia, m, Mub
I have sent myself.

Tumsigha, m/f, Mub
Self made person.

Tutuwan, m, Mub
This is a title often reserved for a Lela flag bearer. See more on the Lela festival in the introduction.

V

Vaana, f, Mub
Death's property.

Vadgasen, m, Mub
There is no medicine that can prevent death.

Vadjemia, f, Mub
Death hates me for no reason.

Vadmagmia, f, Mub
Death has dealt with me.

Vadnyonga, f, Mub
Death has overwhelmed me.

Vaduma, m/f, Mub
Death has revived the matter.

Vagana, m, Mub
Death's cure.

Vagansen, m, Mub
Death has no respect for age.

Vahlenna, f, Mub
Death has abandoned me.

Vajemia, f, Mub
Death dislikes me.

Vaka'a, f, Mub
There are too many deaths.

Vakenna, f, Mub
The arrogance of death.

Vakidla, f, Mub
One's dying mat or bed. Wedding name; refers to someone who'll take care of you until your last day.

Vakunseh, f, Mub
Proverbial; death has no family.

Valegha, f, Mub
A death caused from within the house. Also refers to an increase in the mortality rate.

Valemia, f, Mub
She has died and abandoned me.

Valla, f, Mub
Death.

Valogha, f, Mub
Death has loosened it.

A Dictionary of Popular Bali Names

Valuma, f, Mub
A family overtaken by death.

Vanyonga, f, Mub
Death problems.

Vasagmia, f, Mub
Tormented by death.

Vasigha, f, Mub
Death has left this one for me.

Vasona, m/f, Mub
To die well; he/she has had a good death.

Vasonnseh, m/f, Mub
Death is not good for anything.

Vasoseh, m, Mub
Death is not good.

Vednyonga, f, Mug
She has come to settle family disputes.

Vodla, m, Mub
Matters have ended; this name tends to be given to a child whose mother dies after delivery.

Voma, m, Mub
A child born during the Voma festival or in the month of Vomsoa.

Vomkenna, f, Mub
Title; the wife/child of a member of the Voma cult.

Vudingha, m, Mub
It has turned out to be a spear.

Wabidla, m, Mub
I'm uniting the people.

Wadinga, m, Mub
I'm guarding the flag or door post; I'm gathering spears.

Wadlega, f, Mub
Come together; unite.

Wadjo, (also spelled as **Wadyo**) m, Mug
Watch and you will get it. Seek and you shall fine.

Wadmia, m, Mub
He has made me to be self-conscious.

Wadnyonga, f, Mub
She has gathered problems.

Wadsalla, m, Mub
I am visiting my girlfriend only not for marriage/courtship.

Wagala, m, Mub
Pay a visit to the king.

Wagua, m, Mub
To be unanimous in carrying out an action; it also means he has shut his mouth.

Wakuna, f, Mub
I'm uniting you; a peacemaker.

Walla, m, Mub
Gather. One who gathers.

Waluma, f, Mub
She brings the family together.

Wamia, m, Mub
I have been surrounded.

Wasalla, m, Mub
To gather dirt.

Watmi, m, Mub
Pull together.

Wayigha, m Mub
Navel; that which can't be thrown away. It also means I'm caring for a deserted compound.

A Dictionary of Popular Bali Names

Wobga, m, Mub
Don't divert your plan.

Wobyed, Wobyella, m, Mub
Honour the earth.

Wodla, m/f, Mub
Path.

Wotebba, f, Mub
Cool water, a lover of peace, a beloved one.

Wotla, Mub
Water.

Wubba, f, Mub
I have had enough.

Wubilla, m, Mub
I now have dominion.

Wublegha, f, Mub
Cover the house.

Wubligha, f, Mub
I've shut the door.

Wubnyonga, f, Mub
Do not expose the family secret.

Wubyidla, m/f, Mub
He/she has covered his/her head.

Wubvalla, m, Mub
He has covered death.

Wuvalla, m, Mub,
You have followed death.

Y

Yahdima, f, Mub
Symbolic; a cow's tail; in another sense, it also means a woman who'll make my dancing lively.

Yahnu, m/f, Mug
My own problems.

Yeba, f, Mub
I have no place for a grave near my house.

Yebba, f, Mub
The earth.

Yebduma, m, Mub
The soil's price.

Yebgogha, (Nyamcha, Nyamnsi), f, Mub
Meat for the earth. This name tends to be given to a child whose predecessors had died young.

Yebilla, m, Mub
A traitor; one who ruins the village.

Yebit, m, Mub
Treacherous to the community.

Yebkehmia, f, Mub
The earth has saved me.

Yebkungha, m/f, Mub
The soil cannot fail to be recognised.

Yebkunseh, f, Mub
The earth has no family.

Yebsia, f, Mub
Lightning.

Yekgha, m, Mub
An abandoned piece of land or compound.

Yella, m, Mub
He has been spoilt.

Yeluma, f, Mub
To make a blood pact.

Yemi, m/f, Mub
He/she betrays me; that is, one who releases my secret.

Yethuma, f, Mub
Guinea corn seed.

Yetla, m/f, Mub
Guinea corn seed.

Yevadla, f, Mub
She has forgotten me.

Yevalla, f, Mub
It is a bad death.

Yidmia, f, Mub
I've been forced to agree.

Yidsia, f, Mub
You have forgotten yourself.

Yigha, m/f, Mub
Taking care of a grave; this name tends to be given to a child born after many others have died.

Yissia, m, Mub
He takes pride in himself.

Yiva/Yivalla, m, Mub
Don't yield to death.

Yumbong, f, Mug
A good thing; a beloved one.

Yumnjo, m, Mug
A debt; something that has the potential to cause problems.

Yummun, m/f, Mug
Somebody's gift/ property.

Yummunbia, m/f, Mug
Proverbial; you will reap what you sowed.

Yutiambō, m/f Mug
If you are in want, don't be envious of others' possessions.

Z

Zanvalla, m/f, Mub
Death will see.

Wedding Names

Ajimbom, f, Mug
My wife who knows my wants.

Bosilla, f, Mub
Pride.

Gurkudla, f, Mub
Leopard's skin; symbolises a cherished item. It also means the one who will give me a good name.

Nahbudla, f, Mub
A tall woman.

Nahsadla, f, Mub
A good and befitting woman.

Nahyella, f, Mub
A light complexioned woman.

Ndamnted, f, Mug
A potential lucky charm.

Pehtemma, f, Mub
The one who has stunned me with her beauty. The name also makes reference to divided thoughts.

Sadmia, f, Mub
A woman who befits her husband.

Sadnyonga, f, Mub
I sought this challenge.

Temma, f, Mub
My heart; where I'll pay great attention, lovable.

Vakidla, f, Mub
One's dying mat or bed. A partner one can rely on until one's final days on earth.

Equivalents of Chamba and English Names

Abel, m, **Yissia**
Vanity, breath.

Agatha, f, **Sonna**,
Good.

Allan, m, **Wagua**
Harmony

Alfred, m, **Wadmia (Ngidduwō)**
Good counsellor

Amabel, Annabel, f, **Temma**
Lovable. Worthy of one's love.

Ambrose, Divine, m, **Kehmina**
Of immortals, divine.

Amy, Vida, Norna, f, **Mukonghu**, **Nahsadla**, **Yumbong**,
Beloved.

Andrew, Charles, Andy, m, **Bengyella**,
Manly.

Augustus, Augustine, Austin, m, **Nkoeti**
Venerable, deserving respect.

Augustina, Tina, Augusta, f, **Fongwi**
Conveys the same meanings as Augustus above.

Barbara, f, **Behsena**,
Foreign, stranger.

Barnabas, m, **Bakanu**, **Ngidduwō** (m/f)
Son of exhortation.

Barry, m, **Dinga**
Spear

Beatrice, Beatrix, f, **Nahnyuma**,
Happiness

Benjamin, Ben, Benjie, m, **Kehfun** (m/f)
Son of the right hand i.e. of good fortune.

Casmir, m, **Nwana**
Proclamation of peace.

A Dictionary of Popular Bali Names

Caspar, Jasper, Kaspar, m, **Kehfun** (m/f)
Treasure bringer.

Catherine, Kathleen, Kate, f, **Lennyina**
Pure.

Conrad, Konrad, m, **Dumia**
Bold in counsel.

Constance (f), Constantine (m), **Alobbub** (m/f)
Constancy.

Daniel, Dan, Danny, m, **Lesiga** (m/f)
The Lord is judge

Dominic, m, **Foncham**,
Sunday.

Donna, Martha, Patty, f, **Nina**
Mistress, Lady.

Dora, Dorothy, Dorothea, Nathan, Nathaniel, - **Kennyikob** (m/f)
God's gift.

Edith, f, **Badjangman**,
Happy or rich.

Edmund, Eddy, Eddie, m, **Bidgangha**, **Gangdia**
Happy protection.

Edward, Ned, Neddie, m, **Dobgangha**
Rich guard.

Edwin, Eddy, m, **Nchamukong**
Prosperity or riches.

Emmanuel, Immanuel, m, **Mubuhwō** (m/f)
God with us.

Ephraim, m, **Bobyigha** (m/f)
Fruitful

Eric, m, **Wubilla**,
Sole ruler.

Ernest, m, **Jugha** (m/f)

Esther, Estella, Stella, Essie, f, **Sang**, **Nahsang**,
Star.

Eunice, Victoria, f, **Nyongvodla**
Happy victory.

Felicia, Felicity, Joy, f, **Nyongsangha**,
Happy, happiness, joy.

Florence, Flo, Florrie, f, **Bisangha**
Blooming.

Floventius, m, **Nchamukong**
Blooming.

Frederick, Fred, Frederic, m, **Ganseh**
Peace, rule.

Frieda, Irene, Salome, Winifred, f, **Nahnwana, Wakuna, Bitebba**
Peace.

Gerald, m, **Dingbobga**
Spear wielding.

Gerard, m, **Dingsangha**,
Spear-hard.

Gervase, m, **Wadinga**
Spear servant.

Godlove, m, **Kongninyikob** (m/f)
God's love.

Gregory, m, **Mbembeb** (m/f)
Watcher.

Innocent, m, **Lenna, Mbuhnu**
Innocence.

John, Jack, Johnnie, (m) Jane, Janet, Jeanette, Jessie, (f) **Bongnyikob**, m/f
Yahweh, God is gracious.

Jonathan, m, **Afanyikob** (m/f)
Yahweh has given.

Joshua, m, **Nubitgha**,
Yahweh delivers

Lalage, f, **Guka'a**
Talkative.

Leo, m, **Gua**
Lion

Leonard, Lionel, m, **Guryigha**,
Lion, hard.

Lewis, Luther, Louis, m, **Binyella, Kehbila**
Famous warrior.

Lucius, Lucy, Lucinda, f, **Nahyella**,
Light

Margaret, Maggie, Rita, Marjory, Peggy, f, **Nahnyama**
Pearl.

Mirabel, f, **Andin, Behnyonga**
Wonderful.

A Dictionary of Popular Bali Names

Monia, f, **Leyigha**
Alone, solitary.

Morgan, m, **Foliba**
Sea

Nahum, f, **Ngedtikō**
Consoling.

Naomi, Vivian, f, **Bosilla**,
Pleasant, lively.

Nicolas, Nicodemus, m, **Kehbilla, Kehbuma**
People's victory.

Noel, m, **Nubia**
Birthday

Noela, Natalia, f, **Lima** (m/f)
Birthday

Ottilia, Odette, f, **Kehwalla**
Heritage.

Otto, m, **Dingka'a**
Rich

Patience, f, **Nyonglema, Nyonglemuga**
Patience.

Peter, m, **Bungha**
Rock, stone.

Philomena, f, **Wotebba**
I am loved or strong in friendship.

Ransom, f, Gushua, **Kehmia**
Rescue.

Samson, Sampson, m, **Nyama**
Of the sun.

Common Names

Common Insects

Ant

Ngungang

Butterfly

Ghugha

Cicada

Tonkwet

Cockroach

Mbin

Cricket

Ta tschi

Dragonfly

Ta mbabalang

Dung beetle

Ta mufuhti mbed

Grasshopper

Dzohta

Green grasshopper

Ngen

Housefly

Ndzindzi

Locust

Ngem

Mosquito

Lili

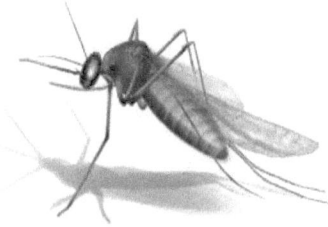

Palm weevil

Mvon

Soldier (army) ants

Ndzed

Stick insect

Ta kongung

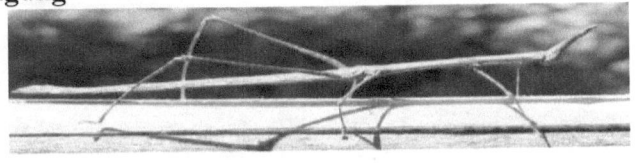

Sugar ants

Bomtita

Termite

Ngo'

Tree ants

Mbinbin

Wasp

Nkonfun

Common Reptiles

Boa constrictor

Ngob nyoo

Fish

Nsu

Frog

Tamson

Lizard

Kubkub

Prawns (crayfish)

Ndzanga

Snake

Nyoo

Toad

Titoh

Tortoise

Kimakoh

Common Animals

Cat

Mu nyangob

Cattle

Nyamtsi

Civet cat (African wild cat)

Muped

Dog

Mvu

A Dictionary of Popular Bali Names

Dwarf cow

Mfong

Elephant

Nswen

Goat

Mbi

He-goat

Mbehmbi

Horse

Nyambani

Leopard

Gu

A Dictionary of Popular Bali Names

Monkey

Nkan

Porcupine

Ngupnyam

Rat

Mbab

Rhinoceros

Ngwanyinyi

Sheep

Ndzombi

Squirrel

dzu'dzusang

A Dictionary of Popular Bali Names

Common Birds

Bat

Lum

Clock bird

Ngohkulok

Cock (rooster, cockerel)

Nkoe ngob

Dove

Mbunghu

Duck

Ngobnsti

Hawk

Nchoh

Hen

Ma ngob

Owl

Nkungdum

Sparrow

Mudzukod

Swallow

Pepe

Wagtail

Kaliwa

A Dictionary of Popular Bali Names

Weaver bird

Nchohbang

Woodpecker

Kukoh mbentu

Wren

Sisi

Common Plants and Fruits

Aerial yam

Ntam

Arabica coffee

Kofi Arabica

Bambara groundnut

Ndzuu

A Dictionary of Popular Bali Names

Bitter kola

Ngandzom

Cocoyam

Nkuh

Guava

Ntam tu

Kola nut

Bi

Maize

Ngafut

Peanuts

Mbiyang

A Dictionary of Popular Bali Names

Plantain

Nkudong

Sweet yam

Ndongbun

Sweet potato

Dzubang

Tobacco

Ndibahg

Yam

Dzu'

www.ingramcontent.com/pod-product-compliance
Lightning Source LLC
Chambersburg PA
CBHW021130300426
44113CB00006B/359